S0-AKC-985

How to NOT plan a Wedding

It's not ALWAYS about the Bride!

Lesley Wise

Copyright © 2017 Lesley Wise
All rights reserved.
ISBN-13: 978-0692836958 (Lesley Wise)
ISBN-10: 0692836950
Library of Congress Control Number: 2017901618
Lesley Wise, Portland, Oregon

Dedication

To all couples trying to navigate the new, arduous, and expensive road to planning a wedding. May your journey be stress-free and your day be beautiful, peaceful, and well managed!

Contents

Acknowledgments

I would like to thank the couples who, over the years, have given me all the stories included in this book, and to all the wedding planning books and guides that gave them the ideas and suggestions that ultimately ended up as stories in this book.

Thank you, Alice Falzone, of MoscaStudio.com for the photo on the cover. And to Hollie and all her girls for the impromptu pose, that was a very fun wedding!

To Carolee and Denise, my very dearest and oldest (in time, not age!) friends and partners in crime, for your grammar, spelling, and content corrections and for translating my confusing (to you) UK English grammar into that funny American English stuff !

Finally, to Jackie and the many other friends who read, corrected, suggested, and gave me their own stories to share. I would not have finished it without you all, or learned all those grammar rules!

Introduction

"My mother says I didn't open my eyes for eight days after I was born, but when I did, the first thing I saw was an engagement ring. I was hooked".

~Elizabeth Taylor

While talking to some friends one day about their longtime relationship, I asked when they were going to get married. Their reply was, "We can't afford to get married right now." This couple already lives together and has a baby, but it's the same for people who are not living together. The engagement promises a wedding of bliss, but the reality of the financial struggle to get there is daunting.

Actually, getting married does not cost that much. It's the wedding that might break the bank, the show that you put on for your guests and family. Once you select the venue, guests, food and drinks, flowers and pictures, the perfect expensive wedding dress, it creates budgetary panic in most brides.

When you started looking at planning your wedding, did you ask yourself; am I the only one who:

- ♥ doesn't know where to start?
- ♥ thinks this is so overwhelming?
- ♥ doesn't want to go broke over this?
- ♥ doesn't want 500 people at my wedding?
- ♥ doesn't want even 50 people!

- ♥ doesn't want the 'destination wedding' my friends are all doing?
- ♥ doesn't want to do what everyone else is doing?

This book is about helping you rethink weddings. Specifically, this is a book to help you rethink planning a wedding. It's a reframing of what a wedding really should be about. And contrary to what popular culture has led us to believe, it's not always about the bride.

I'm not telling you to give up your dream. I'm not telling you that you can't have the perfect image of your special day, which you have been carrying around in your head since you were a little child, daydreaming of your dress and veil.

As a professional wedding specialist, I have been the caterer, decorator, dress maker, photographer, videographer, and planner. When it comes to weddings, I've seen it all; the good, the bad, and the ugly.

I've been in the dressing room when the bride's dress doesn't fit because those last ten pounds never came off. I've been at the reception where a fight breaks out between divorced parents who are still using their kids to hurt each other. Or the best man who had to be escorted from the venue because he drank a little too much! I have watched countless hours of video of blended family dynamics. Wasted food and cake and over the top flowers and decorations end up in the trash.

One of the main reasons I'm writing this book is to have that tough talk no one else is going to have with you about weddings. I will be guiding you through some of the critical decisions that you need to have your dream come true.

Remember, this wedding is not about just the bride, as much as you may want it to be. That's only human. At the end of the day, no matter what your role in the wedding, it's not about you. It's about the big picture. I'm here to help you navigate all the decisions and all the pieces in this incredibly complex puzzle that become a wedding day.

At the time of writing this book, it's 2017. The 21st century has ushered in marriage dynamics that modern history hasn't seen. We've got bicoastal. We've got bipolar. We have mixed religions and mixed beliefs. We are heterosexual, bisexual, gay, lesbian, and transgender. The ceremonies are also just as diverse with religious, secular, spiritual, casual and just plain off the wall crazy. We've got blended families, no families, and fighting families. We've got – just list it out and say, "None of that matters because ultimately the goal is for the day to be special."

All the other books you're going to find on weddings and wedding planning are not going to cover the subjects I'm covering here. If you're looking for information on how to set the table, Martha Stewart has cornered that market. If you're looking for advice about the best dress to wear or what kind of gifts to buy for the wedding party, there are plenty of books on those subjects. What I've set out to do is talk about the things no one else is willing to talk about, the hard topics. The things you do not think about until you realize, often too late, you should have thought about them.

I have tried to make this book a quick read. I am sure you are already overwhelmed by the amount of wedding information there is out there! It is not a planning book. It is a 'think before you plan' book. I am hoping to point out some of the issues that often come up if you do not know that they could.

It's not Always About the Bride

"If you're going to plan a wedding, then a certain amount of suffering is not a choice."

~ Ellie Kemper

I f you have never planned a wedding or have never been to a wedding, you might be in for a shock. Or, if you have only attended a wonderfully perfect wedding and assume they are all like that, you are living in a wedding fantasy. I am not here to burst that bubble. I am here to cover topics you might not even have thought to ask about, or even considered.

Things like:

- ♥ how do you deal with two sets of parents who hate each other?
- ♥ what are the pros and cons of destination weddings?
- ♥ does it really make sense to blow the equivalent of a down payment for a house on a party that lasts just four hours?
- ♥ how many bridesmaids are too many?
- ♥ are beach weddings all they are cracked up to be?
- ♥ is that white dress with the $4,000 price tag really worth it?
- ♥ why do cakes cost so much?
- ♥ DJ or band?
- ♥ some alternative ideas, plus so much more!

By the end of this book, you will have tools to help you:

- ♥ reduce your stress - let go, ask for help
- ♥ keep a 30,000 foot view in mind
- ♥ have fun with your special day
- ♥ put on a successful event everyone will love
- ♥ avoid common pitfalls such as family drama, forgotten components, and timing issues
- ♥ anticipate how long it takes to do something
- ♥ delegate tasks
- ♥ understand the vendor relationship to keep your vendors happy, so they don't ruin your day.
- ♥ discover behind the scenes industry secrets that will help make your day that much better.

If you stay with me, my gift to you is to have a day that's unlike any other. A day that's going to be special and uncomplicated. The result will be one that everybody feels good about and one that you remember with fond feelings rather than resentment and disappointment. Because, at the end of the day, isn't that what you really want?

So how can we make the day as special as possible, given all these circumstances that are bound to occur that are now par for the course?

Keep in mind that a wedding, like any big event, is like an iceberg. As an attendee, all you're seeing is the surface -- everything in place after weeks, months, or sometimes years of behind the scenes work to get it to float.

One of the biggest mistakes people make when it comes to planning a wedding is never moving beyond that surface level. Never taking the time to understand the 90% below the surface.

Let's get started with Wedding Basics 101...

How to Read this Book

If you are at the beginning stages of your planning, you should start with the budget. I have written this book in the order I think is important to consider, although almost everything comes under the budget umbrella, money dictates everything.

If like most brides, you're stuck on one issue or decision, such as trying to decide on a beach wedding or vineyard, you can flip to the chapter on locations or destinations. This section will answer specific questions.

Maybe you are having a hard time deciding who to invite and who to exclude, without hurting feelings. Find clarity in the 'Guest List' chapter or check in on relationships.

There are charts to review, statistics that might surprise you, and suggestions you might not have considered, all dispersed with real life stories from real life weddings I have witnessed as a vendor and as a guest. Some stories also come from the many friends who have been to weddings that also left them wondering.

Who Should Read this Book

"Come on, planning a wedding, let's be honest, it's not fun. It's not fun being in a wedding'."

~Wendi McLendon-Covey

T his is a book primarily written for the bride, but if you are the mother, the sister, the friend, the groom, the best man, or even a seasoned planner, you will play a significant role in the game. You also need to know that a wedding is not always about the bride.

The marriage is about the bride, and the groom hopefully. The wedding, however, is about the guests. You also should consider the vendors you will hire, and the friends and family who will or will not help you. It's about the relationships, the arguments, the peace you are trying to keep, and the money.

The money and costs will be your biggest and most argued about part of the wedding, the marriage, the family and the rest of your life. So, although you can read this book in any order you choose, I suggest starting with the budget section. It's going to be the driving force behind everything else.

The Engagement

"I try to remember, as I hear about friends getting engaged, that it's not about the ring and it's not about the wedding. It's a grave thing, getting married. And it's easy to get swept up in the wrong things."

~Gwyneth Paltrow

- ♥ How to NOT break the news
- ♥ How to NOT think it's all about you
- ♥ How to NOT get swept away in spending too much, worrying too much

He popped the question. You are all giddy with excitement and can't wait to start planning. You look at bridal books, tell your friends, change your Facebook status and then let your parents know. (yes it does go in that order sometimes!)

There are many ways proposals happen, planned and not so planned. You might imagine romantic sky writing or rose ceremonies. Fantasize about swallowing your ring in a Chinese desserts, or at a surprise reunion. On occasion, the proposal, or the even the reply, happens in the spur of a beautiful moment. Then, reality hits and the mind runs with all kinds of questions:

- ♥ What did I just agree to?
- ♥ Is this what I really want?
- ♥ Is he/she truly the one for me, without a doubt, no questions asked?

- ♥ Who will be my best man/maid of honor?
- ♥ Attendants, flowers, photos. Oh my!
- ♥ How am I going to pay for this?

You must have many exciting thoughts and ideas running through your mind, or none.

You may have been planning for this moment for a long time. You both know exactly what you want and are ready to face the wedding planning world. It was a perfect and romantic proposal. You both love each other and want to spend the rest of your lives together, and are willing to do whatever to make that happen.

Wonderful, we are off to a great start!

But, if your first thoughts are of your dream dress, the perfect location, flowers, colors, food, and you can't wait to start, then you need to stop right there and refocus. Are you more interested in the wedding or the marriage?

This is ultimately about marriage, a commitment to the one you are planning to spend the rest of your life with (hopefully) and create a family. It's about the happily ever 'after' the fairy tale.

You might be thinking, "It's the bride's day. It's all about me. The one day I have been waiting for since I first put a piece of white lace on my head and 'married' the boy next door in the tree fort at age six or ten." Or maybe it was the first wedding you went to or saw in a movie, all romantic and beautiful. Well, from the outside it seemed all romantic and beautiful. If you are in that mind set, then we need to reset that mind!

As a bride, you should decide if it's all about you, or all about the guests. The dress is of course all about you, the excitement, stress, anxiety and trepidation is also all about you, but the rest is about your family and friends and all the vendors and services make your day the best it can be.

Tip: If you want this to be all about you, elope!

If you are eloping with just witnesses or a couple of friends, then this is all about the couple. Enjoying each other and the promises. You do still have to think a little bit about the person performing the ceremony, but mostly this kind of wedding is all about the couple.

Now, if you are planning to invite guests, then it becomes more about them. You are throwing this party for your guests. You are putting on a show, for your guests. You want them to watch and enjoy the ceremony and all the toasts and dances and cake cutting. You are thankful thinking of the gifts they will bring.

Your respective families, whether you all get along or not, will also play a huge part in this new life. For good or bad, ups and downs, in sickness and in health and all that.

Of course, we all want to start our wonderful life with a wonderful celebration, something to remember and remind ourselves of the love we are sharing and the family we are joining. We need to make those promises and secure our vows, and of course in most instances, sign the legal stuff. But weddings have become so over the top and out of control that we forget the big picture. The Marriage.

Let's think about the next step before our minds run wild with images of satin and lace and the groom in a sexy tux, because it might be the only time you can get him in a suit!

Listen to each other

Enjoy the news together for a while. Think and talk and discuss and plan and look long term. Decide on who gets the news first. Set the ne for your wedding planning right from the start by slowing down and thinking. Ask each other some questions about what you both want and don't want. It is not all about you. Start with a simple, "What do you want this wedding to be like?" Unless you are both on the same page, and those pages might not be defined yet, there will be problems. Especially money problems.

Amy and John

I came across this story on a wedding forum. John was so excited with a plan to surprise his longtime girlfriend when he asked her to marry him. He bought a very expensive diamond ring, set a romantic stage surrounded by friends and on one knee, presented the ring as he popped the question. Amy's first reaction was total surprise, then reality hit, and she was not happy. Amy went on to explain that he never listens to her. He doesn't know what she likes and never thinks to ask. Apparently, the conversation had come up many times that she is not into large and showy diamonds, surprise events or having lots of fuss showered over her.

Personally, I think this story goes both ways. To me, it was a very romantic gesture. How could Amy not know this about John? He really was a romantic at heart even if she wasn't. You have to give a little in both directions if any of this is going to work.

I am not saying don't surprise your partner with romantic gestures, but know what they want. Understand where their comfort level is and plan accordingly.

Enjoy this beautiful moment together first. Plan a nice time with friends and family to share your great news, then, you can slowly tell the world, because, after that, everyone and their mother will have advice for you.

Speaking of mothers, (and we have a section on that) for the mother of the bride this is also the day they have been waiting for. It's tradition for mothers to help prepare their daughters for marriage, plan the wedding, invite the guests and give them away (well the father does that part). It used to be the bride would go with a dowry of a goat or chicken, or even a castle and all the land if you were lucky enough.

But things have changed. Parents are still helping with planning and costs, but, today, too many parents don't have enough goats and chickens to go around so next in your thinking should be money.

The Budget

"I think a lot of people get so obsessed with the wedding and the expense of the wedding that they miss out on what the real purpose is. It's not about a production number, it's about a meaningful moment between two people that's witnessed by people that they actually really know and care about."

~ Jane Seymore

- ♥ How to NOT borrow and run up the credit card
- ♥ How to NOT buy on impulse -- Exercise the 24-hour rule
- ♥ How to NOT assume you will stay on budget -- Plan for emergencies

The engagement is generally the time you spend planning the wedding and saving the money. It could be a long drawn out, "When are you going to finally set the date?" or the speedier, "Let's get hitched tomorrow." However long the wait time between the proposal and the actual marriage, there are many things to consider and plan.

The very first step to any wedding, or any project that requires spending someone's hard earned cash, is the budget. It's tedious, but necessary. What usually starts most arguments is costs and money. Don't start here.

Be realistic. Figure out how much you have to spend, not what you want to spend. You can have the most perfect wedding, for the least amount of money, with careful planning and research.

Many websites offer budgeting techniques. I suggest you examine creative ways to save money. Off season, mid-week, coupons, stay-cations. There are plenty of options.

Lesley and Rob

My own wedding was held on a friend's beautiful property in the California wine country. Friends and family brought food, arranged flowers, and supplied tables and chairs for the fifty or so guests. We spent $250 for the cleanup crew, because I didn't want my friends doing that, plus $30 for a dress off the clearance rack in a bridal shop. It was the most relaxed and perfect wedding I had ever been to, even though it was my own!

If you don't have access to friends with wine country property or wealthy country club parents, consider parks, beach or private gardens. I love showing off my lovely English garden. It's not huge, but in the summer, it makes for beautiful, intimate parties. You don't need a $10,000 winery tab to create a beautiful scene. Guests should be there to see you not the view. The venue should also complement you and be special to you. Let it set the tone for your day.

Consider locations that speak to your personal likes: Are you a beach lover, prefer the forest, lush green lawns or your parent's backyard? There is more information about choosing locations in logistics and destinations.

TIP- Open a joint banking account to use solely for your wedding purchases. Find a budgeting app or on-line money management program, so you can have quick access as you shop and spend. Deposit any savings, parent contributions and cash gifts to cover your growing budget

Be realistic. Don't get into debt before you start your happily ever after or it will be a Grimm fairy tale. If you do not have the money saved for the dream wedding, then move the date until you do or change things on your wish list.

Make sure you agree who pays for what and budget well. If someone else is footing the bill, consider what strings might come with that. If you are the kind of person that likes to be taken care of and wants it all done for you, and love that someone else is paying for it. Well good for you. But in my experience, that does not happen much and never ends well.

Mathew and Becky

I was hired to videotape Mathew and Becky's wedding. It was a lavish fairy tale affair. The groom's parents, members of an elite country club, were excited to show off their son and new bride to their friends and spared no expense. They planned the event for over a year making sure everything was just right for the perfect wedding. The large and long ceremony was outside on the grounds in lovely weather and the reception in the highly-decorated banquet room. The food was gourmet and free flowing wine, beer and drinks kept everyone happy.

The wedding was just as Becky had envisioned, but Mathew's family paid for it all and planned it all. As Becky and her family did not have this kind of money, she had very little to do with any of the decisions and planning. The jealousy and arguments over money and who was paying started early and the 'this is my son's wedding' attitude was very apparent during the reception. Becky's family left early. The couple divorced one year later leaving a massive credit card debt and angry parents.

This was definitely a case of 'not about the bride,' but it was also not about the groom at this point, it was all about the family who had the money.

The Planning

"People spend more time in planning the wedding than they do in planning the marriage."

—Zig Ziglar

- ♥ How to NOT underestimate a good plan
- ♥ How to NOT miss the bus
- ♥ How to NOT have anything hit the fan

I f you can afford to hire a planner from start to finish and you just show up, and it's done, great.

But you still must plan your trip there. You still must plan your trip back, whether you're getting on a bus or you've got a limo. There's still a certain amount of planning that should be done, even if somebody is taking over the whole day. You still may have to plan the getaway to your hotel. You may have to book your hotel.

Unless you have a personal assistant, who follows you around with a clipboard all day and tells you, "OK, now it's time to come this way. Now it's time to go that way", which is what personal assistants do, you are going to have to do some of the legwork.

We see it in the movies, with the whispering in the ear like in the "Devil Wears Prada." She's telling Meryl Streep, "Oh, this is Mr. and Mrs. so and so." She has her whole book there.

But, this really only happens in the movies. And in the one percent of the one percent, who can afford that.

The reality is, folks – you wouldn't be reading this book if this was you. If you are, great. I would love to have you along for the ride. S**t happens to you too. I don't care how much money you have. There are costs involved in every little detail, and they add up to one big bill very quickly.

Logistics

I don't like the word logistics. It doesn't sound very romantic or magical! But it is what it is! Coordination, planning, managing are all words you typically see connected to 'Wedding.' Logistically, it's logistics that gets it all done.

For example, coordinating the schedules, the guests, the family, and the individuals who are helping you. Other considerations are, where all the equipment goes, how many chairs you need, where does the DJ or music set up, where does the cake sit, and what about the security of all those expensive gifts?

Many wedding venues have event planners/coordinating teams on site. They meet with you, take down all your details, show you a pretty, detailed map of how many tables and chairs you need and where they all go and charge you accordingly. Then magically they are all set up when you arrive, all spaced perfectly for your 157 guests, (confirmed the week before) DJ, bar, food, and cake. They have done this before, know what's needed and where it all goes. You do not have to stress. It's beautiful. The only thing they do not do is coordinate you and your guests. You will need someone for the logistics. And I can never stress enough how important that person will be.

You will soon find that most of the stress starts when you decide to coordinate all these logistics yourself. Chances are, you have not planned a wedding before, and don't really understand how long it takes to move chairs and tables, let alone people! Separating guests from a great conversation is hard! Girls getting their hair and makeup designed always takes longer than the men who spontaneously decide to get the keg, dress, watch a football game, play Xbox, shoot pool, and then get to the venue! Florists, bakers, photographer, officiant, all your vendors who have done this before will be on time, so you had better make sure you have a good logistical plan.

Where to Start

"Falling in love was the easy part; planning a wedding – yikes!"

~Niecy Nash

The kinds of weddings we are exposed to on television and in the movies average six figures and beyond. For example, that wedding made famous in the movie "Father of the Bride" comes in just under $150,000. Probably more today.

Ouch!

For the average family, $150,000 is out of the question for a party that lasts a little more than four hours. According to current surveys, the average cost of a wedding in the US in 2015 was more than $32,000 and 24% of couples never had a budget.

There is also lots of research out there that concludes; the more you spend on your wedding, the less likely the marriage will last! Not sure how true that is but it makes you think, are you willing to spend your money on a great marriage or just a great wedding?

There are many budget generating websites out there, and I encourage you to search for those or use mine as a guide, but whatever you find, first figure out how much money you have or want to spend, then set your budget. To get you started, your ceremony will be about 2% of your budget and your reception about 50%. The rest goes to the dress, clothes, flowers, cars and things you might never have thought about.

Description	2015 National Average Costs	% of Budget	Your Max Budget	Est.	Actual
WEDDING BUDGET WORKSHEET					
Wedding Planner	$1,996				
Rehersal Dinner	$1,296				
Reception	$14,788	50%			
Venue and rentals					
Catering	$68 pp				
Beverages					
Cake	$575				
Miscellaneous fees/tip/service					
Wedding Rings		2%			
Bride's ring, includes Engagment	$6,111				
Groom's ring	$468				
Attire		10%			
Gown and alterations	$1,469				
Headpiece and veil					
Bridal accessories					
Hair and makeup					
Groom's tux or suit	$269				
Groom's accessories					
Miscellaneous fees/alterations/cleaning					
Flowers and Decorations (10 percent)	$2,300	10%			
Floral arrangements for ceremony					
Flower girl's petals and basket					
Bride's bouquet					
Bridesmaid's bouquets					
Boutonnieres and corsages					
Reception decorations					
Lighting					
Miscellaneous fees/tip/service					
Music		10%			
Ceremony Cocktail-hour musicians	$703				
Band, deejay, or entertainment	$1,171				
Sound-system or dance-floor rental					
Miscellaneous fees/tip/service					

Description	2015 National Average Costs	% of Budget	Your Max Budget	Est.	Actual
WEDDING BUDGET WORKSHEET ...continued					
Photographs and Video		10%			
Photography	$2,600				
Video	$1,824				
Additional prints and albums					
Miscellaneous fees/tip/service					
Favors and Gifts	$267	3%			
Welcome gifts for out-of-town guests					
Bridal-party gifts					
Ceremony Fees		2-3%			
Officiant or church donation	$273				
Ceremony site or venue fee					
Miscellaneous fees/tip/service					
Stationery	$445	2%			
Save-the-date cards					
Invitations and RSVPs					
Programs, seating and place cards					
Menu cards					
Thank-you notes					
Postage					
Transportation	$100 hr	1%			
Limousine or car rental for bride and groom					
Limousine or car rental for bridal party					
Transportation for out-of-town guests					
Valet parking					
Miscellaneous fees/tip/service					
TOTALS			0	0	0
REMAINING BUDGET					

Don't assume that your parents can or want to help you. But if you can, sit with each set of parents and ask what, if anything they can contribute or gift to you. Then be realistic on what you can contribute.

Also, do not assume that you will stay within that budget! Have at least a 5%-10% contingency for the emergencies and forgotten.

Whether you just have enough to get by or unlimited cash from your trust fund, the planning rules are the same; The what, where, when, why, who, in no particular order and ending in the How. How the heck are we going to put all this together?

These should be the things to ask for the entire event and all your smaller events and projects within that event. From the pre-parties, dinners, and rehearsal, to the smaller tasks like choosing the flowers, catering, and the day of events. Feel overwhelmed yet?

Let's start small.

The W's

"Plans are nothing; planning is everything."

~Dwight D. Eisenhower

Consider how you work on projects or might plan events. Are you methodical and go one step at a time? Do you like charts, lists, pictures, binders? Do you prefer to work alone or with others to bounce ideas off? Can you visualize the complete event or do you need help or inspiration to get started? We all work and plan differently, so finding ways to get there is sometimes a challenge.

When I plan an event from concept to completion, I first imagine the occasion in its full glory. The people, decorations, equipment, vendors, tables, chairs, and everything in its place, with everyone enjoying it. I cannot always start planning until I see that vision, then I start working backward. Knowing how many people I need to accommodate, lets me know how much room I need and how many tables and chairs will fit. I ask myself, how will the food be served? Do I need permits, parking, places for vendors to unload? I keep making lists, filling in the blanks and establishing a plan of action.

When I plan for others, I do not have their vision yet, so I need to ask many questions. Often, the client does not have a clue what they want or what the event should look like either, so we are often brainstorming together. Not every great idea or suggestion will work, so I keep asking these questions.

Once we have the first few answers dialed in, we add the sub-lists and keep hammering down the W's until we have the final decisions and a good plan. During your W's, if you find yourself hitting a hard stopping point and can't get definitive answers, or it's too expensive, you might want to rethink or eliminate that element or change your direction.

There is no order to the questions, and you might not need to ask all of them, as some answers are implied or apparent.

It's a formula I use to plan any event or project from concept to completion, no matter how large or small the project. I question and dig for information, work out problems until I cannot dig any further. When I have most of the answers, I start the process of bringing all the elements together.

Let's try a scenario.

WHAT?

For this purpose, a wedding. That seems easy enough. But it could also be the rehearsal, the wedding breakfast, the honeymoon. You have to remember that planning the actual ceremony is just one component of the entire wedding and you need to ask the same questions for each item and event.

WHERE? WHEN?

You might already have your perfect location. But that might be affected by the When. If your location is important, choose your location first, then pick an available date. If your 'When' is more important, your 'Where' will be limited.

WHY?

Why the date? Why the location? Why the event?... why, why, why. It might be that you have that special date that is important to you. If that is the case it helps me in my search for a location.

WHO?

This one is easy. The happy couple, right? Yes, but there are many other 'who's' to put on your lists:

Who are your guests?

Who will take photos and video?

Who is your officiant?

Who will be in your wedding party?

Who will do your flowers?

We will come back and work on the details later, drilling down until we have the final answers and the start of a plan. Some elements will change as you go further into the planning process as one thing will affect another, and you will need to make changes. Using this process will ensure that you have covered all the bases and that it all works together. Ever wondered why it takes so long for some projects to get done, like that new bridge in town? Lots of W's to drill down.

Once we have the basics, we can start putting things together. As you work on your list, some answers and questions will be affected by or contribute to other issues and decisions. It is the perfect way to define what is important to you and where you want to spend your money.

You might want to start with, WHAT type of wedding do you want?

The Ceremony

Let's focus on the ceremony for now, as that is usually the most important part of the day, and usually the least expensive.

You should decide on the *type* of ceremony you both want. I could write another book on the traditions and customs of other cultures, and how many couples are exchanging vows and celebrating in a western environment, borrowing elements from each of their countries and beliefs.

Start with identifying the style of ceremony you would like:

- ♥ Traditional Religious: There are rules of your place of worship you should follow.
- ♥ Traditional Religious: Blended cultures and beliefs
- ♥ Traditional Religious: Not so many rules. A more relaxed place of worship.
- ♥ Traditional Secular: No mention of any religion, not in a place or worship but follow the same long time traditions.
- ♥ Traditional Spiritual: A higher power, your own beliefs, angels, Pagan, etc.
- ♥ Your own free-spirited off the charts crazy different.
- ♥ Elopement. Yep, you still should plan an elopement!
- ♥ Other. There is always something we have never seen before.

Your officiant, or the person you choose to perform your ceremony, will help you with choosing and writing the words. There are many 'ready to go' versions and ideas on the Internet that you can use as written, or personalize to your preference.

The traditional western ceremony might look like this:

- ♥ Processional - bridal party
- ♥ Opening words - welcomes and thanks for coming
- ♥ Statement of Intention - the 'I dos.'
- ♥ Vows - standard or personally written
- ♥ Exchange of rings or tokens
- ♥ Reading or blessing - can be from a friend or family member
- ♥ Pronouncement and the kiss
- ♥ Recessional

Other elements are often added depending on religion, culture or personal preferences. I am not going into details here as there are many sites and books filled with ceremony ideas and components. Just ask your officiant.

- ♥ Sand ceremonies
- ♥ Unity Candle
- ♥ Hand and Stone ceremonies
- ♥ Vows to Children
- ♥ Jumping the Broom
- ♥ Breaking the Glass, the list is long.

On the legal side, there are no ceremony rules. All you have to do is prove you can legally marry, get your license, have someone registered with an organization your state or country recognizes to perform legal unions, and witnesses. It seems kinda cold, doesn't it?

So, let's throw a party!

Next, what kind of party you do want? Don't jump straight to the traditionally average 130 guests for cocktails, dinner, toasts, cake, etc. just yet. Don't get swept up in the party without considering your budget, guests, location, and time.

Stop and take a 30,000' view of your day. Narrow down what is important and go from there.

HOW?

Let's put a simple ceremony together.

You are ready to get married in one year. You have your heart set on July 19th because it holds a very special memory for you and you want to hold the ceremony on the beach where you first met, at sunset.

The questioning might start like this.

Q. What are we planning?

A. In this case, a wedding (this is the easy part).

Q. Where do you want to hold your wedding?

A. At the beach.

Q. When do you want this to happen?

A. July 19.

Q. Why do you want to do this? Implied for the wedding but this question will come up again as we drill down.

Q. Who will you invite?

A. Just a couple of friends.

Q. How are we going to pull it all together?

A. I will do it all myself, just wing it and see what happens. - Oh, I hope not!

Q. How much money do you want to spend?

A. We have not thought about that yet. This is the usual answer. But without a budget, you cannot even start to plan the rest.

So now I know we are planning a wedding and I know where and when. I know what other questions to ask.

If you have not planned a wedding before, you might not know what needs to be asked or where to start, so you will like this book. Different events have different sets of questions. Even different weddings have their own issues depending on lots of factors. That comes with experience or a lot of research!

These first few questions start my thought process on how to bring it all together. It also generates further questioning such as why the beach and is the date important and how many people are they inviting.

During my initial research, I find out that July 19th is a Wednesday and as we are choosing the beach I always check the tide tables. The tide will be at its highest about 4:30 PM.

I know that there is only going to be a couple of friends, so I am not worried about lots of guests trying to get off work for an afternoon, midweek wedding, but the high tide might be an issue. I ask a few more questions to make sure all those answers will work together:

> Do your guests know it will be a Wednesday at the beach and will they be able to attend?

> How does the high tide affect your plans to be on the beach?

Being on the actual beach and July 19th are both important so we change the time to sunset, which gives us a little respite from the highest tide point and check that the guests can make the time change. Well, that was easy. Ceremony done! If that's all we were doing, we would be happy. But of course, it's never that easy!

I start drilling down for more information.

> How will you get there?

> Where will you stay?

> Have you arranged photography?

> Who will officiate the ceremony?

> What are your plans for after the ceremony?

You can see we are not quite done adding logistics.

What if it was not so easy? With the same questions, our answers could take us to a Saturday and 30-40 guests. Now you might need to plan some after ceremony activities or a meal.

Q. What are you thinking for after the ceremony?

A. We want to stay local for cocktails and a meal.

Q. What is your budget?

A. We want to keep it under $2000.

You might already notice we have other things to consider. Saturdays are busy days for weddings. We will need to research available venues that can accommodate 35+ people on a Saturday. A budget of $2000 is pretty unrealistic for thirty-five people, (unless you have friends willing to help and donate) even on the beach. Your marriage license and officiant alone will eat up most of the first $500. If you are planning to pay for the guests to eat dinner or have a drink, that will eat up the rest. Then you might want to consider flowers, photos, a room for the night and so on. Are you beginning to get the picture?

Start your planning binder with all the questions, then hit the Internet for research.

The Venue

"The real act of marriage takes place in the heart, not in the ballroom or church or synagogue. It's a choice you make - not just on your wedding day, but over and over again - and that choice is reflected in the way you treat your husband or wife".
~Barbara De Angelis

- ♥ How to NOT cram your guests into one room
- ♥ How to NOT let weather affect your day
- ♥ How to NOT have your vows drowned by sounds of nature

Some breathtaking venues all over the world lend themselves to incredible backdrops for a wedding and your photos. Many couples choose a venue from photos in magazines, recommendations from friends, or those you visited on vacation.

You should consider your venue carefully when you are viewing a location you are not very familiar with. Also, what might work for a vacation spot does not always lend itself to a wedding ceremony. Again, think of your guests, not yourself. But don't choose a venue based on just photos or emotional reasons alone if you want to shoot for the perfect wedding.

There are many factors to consider when looking at your favorite places. Some questions to start with might be: Will all my guests be able to get there easily and how many guests will it hold?

Size Does Matter!

I worked at a resort where the marketing material stated the main ballroom would hold two hundred and fifty guests seated. But when you actually try and seat that many people you can't move around between the chairs and everyone is very uncomfortable. Pay the venue a visit when the room is set for a similar event so you can get an idea of space. It is hard to visualize people seated or dancing in an empty room.

Think alternative seating. Consider adding some cocktail tables for those more casual guests to stand around and chat instead of sitting in a cramped round set for ten.

Michael and Jessica

A recent wedding I attended, as a guest this time, had a combination of cocktail and seated tables. The guest list was long, so regular table seating in this room would have been tight. The room was arranged with larger tables in the center for those who wanted to sit, with reserved seating for family and close friends. Cocktail tables placed around the perimeter allowed others to stand or walk around visiting and chatting casually.

The hors d'oeuvres table was left out the entire evening, and a light dinner buffet was served. Most people I noticed only ate from the hors d'oeuvres and sat or stood at the cocktail tables. These higher tables also allowed guests to see what was going on closer to the action!

Historic Buildings

I love historic buildings. I like to visit and wander through them at leisure, enjoying the history. I imagine life two hundred or even nine hundred years ago, (if you ever visit Europe!) but then I like to leave after a short time. A brief visit is what most people do when looking at these sites for events. Once you spend a couple hours with a hundred or so guests, things start to change. You do this in the middle of a hot summer, and they change again.

Many of these buildings do not have air conditioning. Some do not even have windows that open for a breeze. Time to consider your guests! If you are squeezing one hundred and fifty of your favorite people into a two-hundred-year-old room, things are going to get hot before the drinks and dancing begin.

Some of the historic buildings have installed airflow; usually, large fans systems or air conditioners have been added later. The nature of these structures cannot always hide the noise these systems create. I notice them mostly because of watching and editing sound on video. Make sure you look and listen for equipment that might need to be turned off during the ceremony, so your guests can hear clearly and any sound recordings are not catching interference.

Garden Weddings

From the large estate gardens to the private backyard, who doesn't love a garden wedding! They do come at a price for all that manicured landscaping or free if you happen to know someone with a lovely outdoor space.

But, these are not without their challenges either. When planning outdoor venues, look beyond the lawns, landscaping, and views and anticipate the inevitable; weather and noise. Seems simple but there are many elements of an outdoor space you might not realize until you need that quiet fifteen or twenty minutes for the ceremony.

ANTONIO AND STACEY

Their wedding was set in a lovely garden high in the hills with fantastic views, waterfalls, flowers, mountains, trees, you name it. The expansive lawn area had plenty of room for the seventy-five seated guests. Under a pre-installed canopy everyone would be shaded from the hot, late summer sun during dinner. The ceremony area was placed further out with a view of the snow-covered mountain in the distance. Stacey entered from the large house and was guided around the waterfall and down a green mossy slope to her waiting groom. It was planned to be picture perfect.

But, the guests were now sitting and sweltering, looking west into the afternoon sun. Although the mountain backdrop was beautiful, the glare from the setting sun was blinding the guests and made photography and video hard to manage. The waterfall, although magnificent, drowned the voices from the couple and officiant, who was not wearing a mic.

Had I been at the planner and at the rehearsal I could have suggested some changes. The huge garden certainly had other options. Quite often, the rehearsals are held at a different time of the day than the actual ceremony, just as this one had been. Stacey had been doing all of her own planning and lacking experience with outside logistics, missed listening for annoying sounds or to consider sun position and occasional breezes. Check where the sun will be at the time of your vows, the view is not so nice if your guests are squinting into the sun.

For small intimate gardens where you have neighbors, you have other potential problems to plan for. Normally small gardens have smaller guest lists. But, even if you have twenty-five people you might have to find parking for maybe twelve additional cars. Is there street parking near the home? Can you arrange the use of a local church, school or commercial property to park for the day?

Then there is noise! Neighbor noise, and your noise if your party is going to 'party' later.

John and Lisa

I officiated a friend's wedding in the family garden on a holiday weekend. It was a small neighborhood garden with lovely landscaping and very private. Earlier in the day, a neighbor decided to power wash his house. Luckily, after a quick explanation by the mother of the bride, the neighbor was done in time before the guests were to arrive. We had just started the opening words when another neighbor to the right decided to use his power saw. A guest quickly jumped up and ran next door to ask for some time, and they were also kind enough to stop. As we started to read the vows, yet another neighbor started up his power washer! We paused again to ask for just ten more minutes. It's nice when you know and get along with your neighbors. John and Lisa took it all in stride, we had a good laugh, and the family sent over cake after.

Just another one of those things you don't think about until it's happening. On any other day, these interruptions in the quiet neighborhood would not have been noticed, or at least not impacted your day too much. A quick note or request to your neighbors that you are hosting a wedding, with the dates and times. If they are planning any home improvements on that day, they will be happy to schedule around your twenty minutes of ceremony. Or just invite them!

This goes for the country estates too; larger gardens have bigger and noisier equipment!

I have been in lovely homes and gardens that back onto main roads and interstates or in noisy commercial areas near businesses with people working. Locations near rivers and water features offer a beautiful sound until you are trying to talk or listen.

I worked a wedding that was planned the same weekend as an international airshow and directly under the flight path! Talk about a noise challenge! Guests also didn't know whether to watch the ceremony or the fighter jets that happened to fly with precision and perfect ceremony timing.

Brian and Rachel

I attended a lovely garden wedding at a popular venue. It did come with an onsite planner, but I am not sure exactly what guidance and planning information was given to the couple.

The venue had multiple ceremony sites to choose from, both with and without water features. The weather was lovely this day with a gentle breeze. There was no microphone or sound system provided, and the officiants' very soft voice disappeared on the breeze. Not one person, other than the couple, heard a single word of that ceremony. I could see people trying to listen, talking and complaining to each other and clearly frustrated.

In my opinion, this was something the venue's sales person should have suggested or provided. The sound is not something most couples consider when renting an outside facility that has an onsite planner.

Look and listen when you are visiting sites and ask questions. While you are taking photos for your planning book, use your phone to record the ambient sounds to remind you later of how quiet or noisy it was. You can then decide if you will need amplified sound or a loud speaking officiant! As the officiant, I do not like to shout to guests while competing with waterfalls or traffic.

The Destination Wedding

"Follow what you are genuinely passionate about and let that
guide you to your destination."

~Diane Sawyer

- ♥ How to NOT have your guests go broke
- ♥ How to NOT miss the boat
- ♥ How to NOT get lost in translation

D estination weddings come in all shapes and sizes. A quick drive to the closest national park or a long plane trip to the most exclusive of white sandy beaches with aqua-clear palm tree bordered seas.

For that matter, I am not sure if it's because people want the romantic and exotic scenery or they just don't want anyone to go to the wedding!

When you plan a destination wedding, think about who you want to celebrate with you. Then, who can afford to go? If you do just want to elope and bring a couple of friends, that is great. It's romantic and personal; it can be beautiful. It would be my choice. I love small intimate weddings whereever they are.

But if you do want friends and family to be at your wedding, consider these issues: Can they afford a trip to some exotic faraway place? Do they want to go? Are parents or grandparents able to travel or fly?

A couple I knew planned their wedding on short notice. With hearts set on a romantic beach setting in a favorite overseas resort, booked the trip and invited the guests. Without enough time to plan for an overseas trip, many of the guests could not attend. Those who felt obligated to go, parents, close friends, and family, scrambled to make plans and others felt left out, slighted, and thought the short notice invitation was inconsiderate.

If you are going to plan a destination that requires long travel times, go by yourselves and get married on the beach of your dreams. Then, come back and schedule a time for your friends and family to celebrate with you. Or give a couple of years notice so people can save their money and plan ahead. We all love an excuse for a vacation!

Destination Beach

We love the sound of the ocean, but beach weddings have their own set of problems. Whether it's your local beach or a tropical oasis, they can also have unpredictable wind and waves, screeching birds, people playing and kids screaming, to name a few.

If you are lucky enough to find a quiet and private beach some of those people noises will go away, but maybe not the wind and waves.

Often, there is no power for sound amplification, and although you could bring a small portable system, your voice is still going to travel and compete with the wind. For those intimate beach weddings, where formal seating is not an option, I like to gather the guests close in a circle surrounding the couple. It helps to keep the voices more audible and the other sounds out.

Know your beach, know the weather, have a plan b, and c. If you can visit the beach for a trial run on sound and weather, choose the same time of day to test the sun position and of course the tides.

Or, better still, take your wedding into a controllable environment and just have your photos taken outside. Guests don't care if they are looking at the ocean or a wall during the ceremony, they will be hopefully watching you and will have plenty of time to enjoy the views later.

Javier and Dominque

On a Pacific Northwest beach in mid-summer, the location offered a beautiful view of the Pacific Ocean from high above the beach. Although there was a perfectly adequate indoor facility, the couple opted for the outside ceremony site and tented reception area.

As guests arrived, they huddled close to the tent to keep out of the cold wind that had picked up, or for fear of being blown down the cliff face. The insistence of having the perfect view of the ocean did nothing for the ceremony and the freezing guests, but the ceremony went on albeit rushed and teeth chattering. The guests could not hear the words being spoken during the ceremony and could not wait to get out of the wind.

The tent, with its plastic windows offering a distorted view of the ocean, was almost blowing off the cliff, the sound of the wind whipping the sidewalls and catching the roof made it nearly impossible to hear anything inside. Conversations, toasts, and speeches were blown out to sea. Editing video later, it was impossible to correct the sound the wind obliterated.

Conditions and Accessibility

Getting to the beach is also a challenge sometimes. For most of your guests, a beach wedding requires travel. It might be an hour or two, or an international flight. Consider how feasible it is for everyone to get there and how much work and money you want it to be.

You might find it easy to scale a rocky trail to get to the private cove you found, but can your guests? I have hiked numerous trails to get to those remote and secluded beaches for a fifteen-minute ceremony. Not fun. Sometimes I think I should charge danger money just to get there! Again, it's not always about the Bride.

When you choose your beach, check if local rules allow you to hold a wedding on public beaches, and what you can and cannot do. Some do not let you set up chairs, have amplified music or large groups. The local Chamber of Commerce, Parks and Rec or city permit departments can help.

For the hotel or resort beach weddings, you can hand most of the logistics to the onsite planner. Be aware, though, this is just a sales person for the resort who will make sure you have food and drinks for a hefty price, and the rest is up to you. Domestic locations are easier to deal with, but international destinations take more work and time. You might have to get passports, flights and sometimes visas, which means so do your guests. You might also be working in different time zones and experience language barriers. Again, know your beach, know the conditions, know the rules, know what can go wrong.

Chris and Riley

A couple planned a wedding in a small town in Baja, Mexico and traveled ahead of their guests. We were also scheduled to visit there the same week but a hurricane headed inland canceling all flights and leaving us at the airport, with the entire wedding party, families, photographer, and officiant. Of course, no one made it to the wedding on time.

Although you can't always predict weather situations, they should have at least considered the possibility of flight delays when flying to a remote town in Mexico, during hurricane season. Everyone was booked to fly out the day before the wedding leaving not much room for error or delays.

They also had to get from the airport to the town and from the town, on a boat, across the sea to a remote island with everything on the boat. Not sure after that what happened but apparently it did not go as planned.

Had they asked a few more questions during the planning stage, and considered all possible scenarios with an overseas destination, they could at least have added an extra day just in case. Sometimes, these things are unavoidable, but at least add a 'plan b' so you are not scrambling and stressing at the last minute.

My suggestion for a faraway destination is to get everyone there first, Plan the vacation part first with the wedding a few days or a week later. It also gives you plenty of time to deal with issues that might present themselves once you have arrived.

Even close to home there can be trouble if you do not plan ahead.

Mathew and Amanda

I was hired to officiate on a beautiful beach in the Pacific Northwest. As always, I checked the tide tables, and they did agree to adjust the times to make the most of the low tide. The popular ceremony site requires walking around a point that is only accessible at low tide. I also informed them that access to this beach is difficult with rustic steps down a rocky incline before reaching the sandy shore. They had been there before, but I do not think they actually paid attention to the access as it was not an issue for the young couple.

On arrival, most at their wedding party were elderly, with one in a wheelchair! The guys in the wedding party rigged up a contraption like an ancient chair litter, so they could carry Grandma down these broken steps across a pebble beach and then around the point to the location they had chosen. Now we only had a certain amount of time before the tide comes in and you have to navigate back around the rocks, or you're cut off.

Personally, I do not like planning beach weddings, even tropical ones, as they are unpredictable. Also, if it's remote, access can be a problem for some. It's not just the flying, it's once you've arrived. Some of these getaways are very remote. There might be some treacherous roads or in some cases, none at all. Will you need a car, boat, pony and trap, or dog sled?

Cameras do not much like sand either, especially if it's windy. A lot of photographers and videographers will not shoot in windy and sandy conditions.

Those lovely photos you see in the magazines are staged to perfection on calm, warm days when the sun is in a perfect position, or they have a large crew holding lights, reflectors and wind machines. Don't fall for that.

There are so many things to consider when planning a destination wedding, whether you have to fly or you're just going to the local beach. If you do not have a professional planner, do your homework.

If you really must have a beach wedding, consider lake and river beaches or elope! If it's just the two of you, then it works. You only have yourself, a couple of witnesses and the officiant to worry about.

Nick and Lauren

This young couple were very much in love, in a long-distance relationship and juggling school and life. They decided to marry during one of their rare meet ups alone and without the drama of friends and family. With me as their officiant, we went to their favorite beach where they had first met and on a bright and sunny but freezing November day, we walked out onto the sand and asked two strangers to be witness the ceremony. It was a short and sweet and using their camera, I captured a few photos, signed the license, and wished them both well. Even the witnesses were thrilled and enjoyed the random moment. I will always remember that couple and that day. It was romantic and special. Who needs all those bells and whistles when you just have love?

The Guests

"I love dress shopping, and I love talking about the wedding food. That's what makes me happy. If you tell me to do a guest list, I cry. I hate it."

~Chrissy Teigen

- ♥ How to NOT invite everyone
- ♥ How to NOT offend someone
- ♥ How to NOT follow tradition

Part of the budgeting process is knowing how many people you can afford to invite; how many you want to 'entertain' and what mood or tone you want your wedding to take on. Your location, city, state or even country, will also dictate your costs; Some facilities have minimums and maximum guest counts.

You should ask yourself what type of party you see yourself and guests enjoying? Can you imagine five hundred guests or just fifty? Maybe you want a small intimate dinner with just a few friends and family, or, rock it out at a loud and fun dance party with everyone you ever knew!

You don't have to follow tradition here either. Think outside the box.

If you have a lot of friends and family that like to help organize gatherings, there are a lot of ways you can use them and call in some favors. I do suggest you read the section on relationships first! There are some people you should work with and some not so much.

While growing up, my family weddings were usually all 'our' family and not very many 'their' family. Very one sided! But then we did all the work, we were very good at planning and working together, and costs were kept to a minimum. More so from necessity than choice.

Hopefully, you can balance your guest list better. Don't think you need to invite everyone to everything. If you have a few hundred friends on both sides of your guest list, it will be a challenge to decide who to leave out more than who to invite. If you have the budget for a five hundred count guest list, I'd like to be at that party, but, can you realistically thank and visit with that many guests in four hours? Also, could you manage an event where you have to entertain five hundred people? You'd need a team of coordinators!

Grant and Beth

I worked a wedding where the couple had many friends between them. They were both on college teams and very, very popular. They both also had an equally large family circle. Of course, they wanted everyone to attend, and everyone wanted to celebrate with them, but they were trying to stay within budget.

They solved the issue creatively by inviting two hundred and fifty of their immediate family, and closest friends to the ceremony and dinner then opened the evening for dancing and desserts to all who wanted to attend and wish them well.

This fun event would have been a good time to use technology had it been more available. Today you can have ceremony videotaped and played at the reception. The couple will also get to see what they missed too!

You do not have to have a guest list of five hundred to make this work. Elopements can make the most out of this idea. Invite family only or family and closest friends for a nice intimate dinner, then open the party for the cake and dessert. And a no-host bar.

Another good reason for a split event is you can visit easier with those closest to you and elderly members of your family, who might not be too interested in the loud 'disco' later, could retire early after a wonderful long day with you.

The Guest Lists

Compile separate guest lists. I suggest three; those who would drop everything and drive many miles to be there for you. Those who would like to come but might have other commitments; work, family, distance, preventing their attendance, and, those who will only attend if they have nothing better to do!

It is very frustrating when you invite people, they RSVP, then never show up. You could be paying up to $100 per person for a fully catered reception and all the rentals. If just five of your invited guests are no shows, you are out $500.

Venues ask for a final guest count one week before your date. Make sure your guests understand the importance of an RSVP, especially if you are providing a plated meal, and make it easy for them to do that. Enclose a return response card or an online RSVP link to one of the many wedding websites you can create for your event.

The Plus One

Then there is the 'plus one!' Another tricky invite and always up for much discussion. If your budget is tight, I don't think it's necessary to arbitrarily invite people you don't know, even sometimes, people you do! My thoughts on this are; if you have to add 'and guest' to the envelope, don't invite them.

If the guest is a family member or close friend with a serious plus one, at least ask for a name, so they feel personally invited. Or explain to your guest that their 'plus one' is welcome to attend for dessert and dancing and have them suggest the invitation. You might get some push back but stick to your budget and list.

The Parents

Let parents bequeath to their children not riches, but the spirit
of reverence.

~ Plato

- ♥ How to NOT have power struggles
- ♥ How to NOT alienate the Mothers
- ♥ How to NOT forget the Fathers

Traditionally the Bride's parents paid for most or all, of the wedding. They also invited the guests, with their names being first on the invitation, and hosted the reception. The groom's family often hosts the rehearsal dinner.

Today, many couples pay for everything, and if you are the 'throw tradition out the window' type person, decide who might be writing the checks, running the budget and ultimately, the guest list.

Whatever your chosen roles are for each member in the 'planning' of your day, don't let it start with power and influence vs. money. If you and your families are sharing the expenses, then you will need to delegate, diplomatically and delicately, who is responsible for what.

One thing the fathers both have in common is the pride and love for their 'now grown up' child and they like to brag and show them off, whether they show it publicly or not. That is what they are thinking. Sometimes embarrassingly so!

Dads love to give their daughters away. The Fathers of the Groom love to pat the backs of the sons and give the 'atta' boy! If that's all they like to do, let them have that. We all know the planning and the fancy stuff is for the women folk! If you have a father or that male figure who likes to get involved, by all means, let them do what they are good at. But don't let them be forgotten. Remember, most men don't share their feelings like the girls or ask questions (or ask for directions!), that is just how they are wired. So, go with however they are wired. Give them a job with very specific step by step instructions. Write them down or send the instructions to their phones. They can refer to that instead of feeling like they need to ask but can't bring themselves to.

The mothers, now there is a different story. Even I will tread lightly here! There can be conflicts, or not.

Do the mothers get along? Could they work together? Have they even met each other? Often today's parents are meeting for the first time at the wedding! I don't recommend that. Please let the families meet before you do all this. If you think you are just simply marrying each other, you most definitely are not! Each one of you is marrying into whatever 'family' the other has, warts and all. But that is an entirely other book!

We all have heard the 'mother-in-law' stories and scenarios, and not just from the men. I have many mother-in-law stories from pre-planning to the day-of, or just complaints from the couples that they are tired of his mom this and her mom that. Don't start your married life with family drama. You have plenty of time and family gatherings for that.

Apart from the traditional roles above, decide between the two of you whose mom has what strengths and what they can do to help, if they even want to. Some moms just want to be invisible, and some are great with just going to the spa and greeting the guests holding a Cosmopolitan. Nothing wrong with that, guests need greeting and spas are awesome! Take them both out to lunch, or a Cosmo, for a planning date. Make a list of what either one might want to help with and let them choose what they want to do. Of course, you might have to be the delegator if they start looking at each other over the cocktail with narrowing eyes. If the daggers come out, go back to the traditional roles and blame 'They' because that is how 'They' do it! Or hire an event planner.

There are the personal roles that should be delegated to one or the other. Shopping for the dress, primping and planning the bridal finery is mostly left to the bride's mother figure. Sometimes the groom's mom is just so in love with the choice her wonderful son has made, she wants in on everything. If you are on good terms with the overly affectionate in-law, great, but if not, set boundaries and thank and appreciate what they can bring to the planning. Again, it's not always about the Bride!

Jay and Marie

A battle of the moms happened at a friend's wedding. We were invited as guests and offered to produce the video for them as a gift. When you are behind a camera, you are a fly on the wall. You get to see everything, often unknown to the people in the room. Sometimes you don't even know what you are capturing until you go back to edit. The subtle eye rolls when something was suggested, the conversations between others unaware of a rolling camera. It's my very own personal reality show! (We do edit out negative drama for the benefit of the couple). Yet another great argument for the bride to have a 'person.' The one who filters all this drama away from her.

In this instance, Marie was obviously upset. She was pacing and fuming and yelling at everyone in her wake. Meanwhile, I am trying to film the supposedly fun and intimate festivities of getting ready with friends. Her bridesmaids had made excuses to leave the room and while trying to calm her down, learned that a true battle of the moms was playing out somewhere in the building. Both were very strong-willed individuals, both very much the in-charge type of person. They were arguing about whose role it was to greet and seat the guests between the many brothers and sisters in the two families. Marie had asked her brothers to handle it to have them feel involved, and Jay's mom had decided they were not taking it seriously enough and wanted everything to be perfect. I do not think Jay or any of the men knew or cared what was going on as they were all outside playing kickball in their tuxedos! The moms were mad at that too! But boys will be boys! It was a clear case of not enough planning and delegating before the day rather than a mother vs mother thing. Luckily the boys, who don't think much about the planning stuff, all went and did what was instructed of them, still not knowing about, or maybe staying out of, the mom feud! It was an hour or so of unnecessary worry for Marie and the two mothers and could have easily been avoided.

The Blended Family

"When I look back at the pictures of our blended family the day Vince and I married, he and I are smiling, and all the children are frowning."

—Amy Grant

- ♥ Do NOT expect that all family members will embrace your news
- ♥ Do NOT overlook the ramifications of excluding steps and exes
- ♥ Do NOT forget not everyone shares your faith or beliefs

I t's the "I-hate-her-I-hate-him" wedding. When you have blended families, you usually have blended problems. In an ideal world, everyone involved in the marriage gets along famously.

However, the reality is you often find two sets of parents who don't see eye to eye. And when you add into the mix ex-wives, ex-husbands, step siblings, new boyfriends and girlfriends of ex-wives and husbands, you don't have a simple event on your hands, you have a circus.

Family drama makes a great case for elopement, but I will cover that in a different section.

All kidding aside, you can see how the planning can easily get out of control when so many people are involved. When people are getting along, you don't notice it. Everything works. There's no drama. It's when people don't get along that everyone notices.

The Best Friend

"It's easy to impress me. I don't need a fancy party to be happy. Just good friends, good food, and good laughs. I'm happy. I'm satisfied. I'm content."

~Maria Sharapova

- ♥ How to NOT have your friends go broke
- ♥ How to NOT stress out your friends
- ♥ How to NOT out do the friend

If you are a person with lots of friends of marrying age it can become a financial burden once you all start planning weddings. Dresses, shoes, parties, trips, gifts. It adds up fast.

During the first stages of planning, have a heart to heart with your besties, after all, if they are your besties, you can have this heart to heart. Don't assume that all is well on the financial front for any of them. It usually is not. Most single young adults can barely make rent these days. Be sensitive to financial strains when you are asking for their support and involvement.

Mary

Mary is a very popular young lady with a large and equally popular group of girlfriends. She was a chosen bridesmaid for one of her best friends. It was to be a large and over-the-top production. The fairy tale! The first wedding in the group and friends went all out and spared no expense to please the bride, look good in all their finery and have a great party. Not long after, a second girl of the group announced their date, followed by a third. Back to back weddings often happen within large groups of friends, and large families I might add.

In the second wedding, Mary was asked to be Maid of Honor. A great honor itself, but comes with a certain amount of responsibility. After a few weeks of planning, Mary realized she was in over her head and could not afford what the bride was asking of her. This second friend to start planning was trying to live up to or outdo the first wedding, which also happens. This second wedding was looking to be very expensive, and tensions started early. Mary, not wanting to disappoint her friend or even tell her she was struggling, started to resent the expenses she thought were expected of her. She also had the third wedding on the horizon. It was difficult for her to explain her dilemma to the bride and started getting sick and making excuses for why she was not helping. This also started tensions between the entire bridal party.

Try not to put such a burden on your friends, even if they seem to be OK with it. If you start noticing a little apprehension or change in mood and excitement, stop, think and ask. Offer to share some of the expenses of the bachelorette parties, expensive dresses, gifts, and celebrations. Again, this is your production, but it's not all about you.

Your Person

The bride needs to find the one person that's close to her and who can be her advocate, her sounding board, her bodyguard, and her person. Someone, who will protect his or her energy from all the chaos and drama.

It could be the mother, an aunt, a cousin, best friend, mentor at work. It just needs to be a person who you trust to make decisions on your behalf and filter out all the noise and nonsense. Regardless of who you choose, it needs to be made crystal clear to everyone that this person is respected. Any decisions, ideas, suggestions, complaints are run by this person before it gets to the bride.

It can also go for the groom too. It's not always about the bride! Sometimes the groom gets walked all over, and they are often not as vocal as us girls! Do not underestimate their quiet moods. They also need a person.

It could be the hired event planner. But paid or not, that person holds all the power when it comes to final decisions and protecting the bride.

The Children

- ♥ How to NOT have cranky kids
- ♥ How to NOT stress out the kids
- ♥ How to NOT miss a kid moment

Kids are cute at a wedding, sometimes! If the couple getting married have children, they are usually very much part of the ceremony, and depending on the age of the children; there are things you can do, or maybe should not do, to include them.

Children under three, invited to be part of the ceremony, have no idea what is going on. It's not fair to the child or the person having to care for that child when they get tired and cranky. If it's important for you to have these little ones be part of your wedding, and you or the parents would like to enjoy the day, hire a nanny or sitter to take full responsibility for them and make sure they are kept on their schedule.

Having the younger children and babies attend a wedding is mostly for the couple or other family members, not for the benefit of the children so limit their time at the event. If you must have them in the photos, schedule a quick time between naps and food in a quiet place away from distractions and onlookers. Do not plan on them cooperating in front of the camera around your schedule. We know that never happens! Better still, get those family photos at another time, before or after the wedding when there is less excitement to distract them. Kids being kids might be funny to the parents, but your guests or the photographer might not want to wait for them to smile at the stranger behind the camera on cue.

The over three-year-old, especially those invited to be a flower girl or ring bearer might be more aware of what is going on but more interested in dressing up like a prince or princess for the day. Still, do not underestimate their young temperament. They get bored and cranky quickly. Young boys dressed in tuxedos get fidgety if the clothes are uncomfortable and ill-fitting. Imagine yourself in an outfit that is stiff and too large even to look comfortable. They also get really stressed and cranky if they have been told repeatedly to behave a certain way. "Don't get the clothes dirty". "Remember to do this and that and walk here and say that". It's all just too much. Even the grown men hate wearing a rented tux for the most part, and their jackets are off more than on.

The Melt Down

At one wedding, I was video capturing the bridal party getting ready and the guest arrivals. The couple getting married had their niece and nephew, seven and three, as flower girl and ring bearer. The three-year-old was a ham and goofed about while everyone was getting ready and guests started arriving. Happy as a lamb, he didn't know what was going on, but he knew it was fun and lots of people paid him lots of attention. He was lapping it all up then crashed hard in the corner of the altar just before the ceremony. In this instance, no one cared much and just left him there! It was quite cute.

The seven-year-old was quiet and refined and looked lovely in her beautiful dress as she smiled and nodded and greeted guests with Grandma. She was a picture of happiness and ready to honor her important role of scattering the rose petals and standing with the grownups. As the processional started, she took her position and burst into tears. She had been holding it together for so long that the stress was now just too much. She walked down the aisle sobbing her heart out. I am sure it was traumatic for her, but no one seemed to care, considering it cute and funny. No one comforted her no one thought to hold her hand and walk with her.

When you are watching a wedding through a lens, you see and are looking for, events and happenings others may not always be aware of. This young girl had been holding it together for everyone for a good three hours. She seemed like she was having fun but looking back at the video during editing, you can see her on the verge of a meltdown more than once. It was just too much, and she lost it at the most important part!

The Flower Children

Now, this was funny, so I had to include it. It still makes me laugh today. Two siblings, as flower girl and ring bearer again, maybe two and four, were getting ready to walk down the aisle. We had the cameras rolling, and the bride was just about to enter preceded by the young boy and girl. As if on cue, the small boy snatched the basket of petals from his sister, tipped them all over the floor and with such great flare stomped on them over and over again. It was funny. The bride and groom also thought it amusing, and everyone had a good laugh.

Well, except the flower girl who was livid and beating on her brother. This is one of those moments you are glad you included video in your planning!!

If you want your ceremony to go smoothly and you include children, do not expect it to be perfect in any shape or form!

Other People's Children

Including children on your guest list is always a touchy subject, especially if many of your guests or close family have them. These little energetic entertainers can be amusing while tearing up the dance floor during dinner and toasts, but don't feel you have to invite them if kids are not your thing yet. If you do love other people's children and want them to attend, don't assume they will all behave nicely. We all have friends or family with kids who are not that nice to have around!

Again, hire a sitter or nanny or two to manage these little guests. They need structure and lots to do or a nice long movie. Provide healthy snacks and comfortable, quiet places to rest or nap.

If they are getting up to mischief, and the younger ones will, like sticking fingers in the cake, or laying on the floor in a sugar coma, make sure the camera is catching it for later embarrassment when they too are getting married!!

Capturing the Moments

"One of the best ways to make yourself happy in the present is to recall happy times from the past. Photos are a great memory-prompt, and because we tend to take photos of happy occasions, they weight our memories to the good."

~ Gretchen Rubin

- ♥ How to NOT have bad photos end up on Facebook
- ♥ How to NOT show your true colors
- ♥ How to NOT miss those perfect moments

Technology is almost a given at weddings today. It seems like all the guests are photographers, videographers, and DJ's. With cell phones and tablets sticking up through the crowds during all elements of the day and iPods loaded with the latest dance music, who needs a posse of professionals?

Personally, I would like to enjoy the event live, not try and view it through a four-inch screen. When I perform a ceremony, I prefer that the guests do the same. Everyone should be able to enjoy the celebration without the distraction of mobile devices and cameras, but that call is up to the couple and how those interruptions might affect their moment. But, it's not the couple who are affected; they only have eyes for each other. There is nothing more annoying than someone in front of you sticking a screen in your face while you are trying to enjoy the moment. I think it's rude.

You can ask your guests for a cell phone/camera free wedding. Put a small sign near the sign in book or on the guest table. Request that they enjoy the celebration with you without the distraction of technology and make sure you add some humor, letting them know there will be plenty of time for photos, Facebook and Instagram later. Secure and list a hashtag so they can share their photos on-line after the event. I offer a time after the ceremony, right before the recessional, for everyone to take part in a 'Paparazzi Moment.' It adds a fun element to the festivities and allows for some great shots from your professional photographer of everyone with their phones in the air pointed at the couple.

Guest Photographer

Capturing video is challenging enough without having to dodge wannabe photographers. During a ceremony, my husband was getting close-ups of the couple, and I was on the second camera in the back behind all the guests, and next to the hired photographer, catching everything else. Suddenly, during the most important elements of the ceremony, a guest stood up and started taking photos. She was in my direct line of site for filming the couple and blocked my shot completely. Being on a tripod with the best possible vantage point, I could not just pick up and move and was not close enough to ask her to sit. The photographer eventually reached her, also missing some valuable shots, but not before about three minutes of the ceremony was lost. The guest was completely oblivious to us and the other guests she was also blocking.

For those savvy couples who are into the technology thing, work it for all it offers. You can live stream and tweet and share any and everything as it happens. Of course, you will want someone to do that for you. It's not very polite for the couple to be posting on Facebook during the ceremony! If you do have guests and family who cannot make the wedding, there is no reason they can't attend virtually.

For simple Facebook live streams, Skype, Instagram, and other media, ask your favorite teen to help. They are often more comfortable watching life through a lens than fidgeting in a seat during the ceremony. Make sure you have a strong signal where you are, especially for good video. For a more professional setup or a Facetime/Skype scenario, ask your videographer for help.

Preserving the Memories

"Take care of all your memories. For you cannot relive them".

~ Bob Dylan

- ♥ How to NOT forget the day
- ♥ How to NOT miss that perfect shot
- ♥ How to NOT wish you had hired that professional

I think one of the most important things about weddings (other than the marriage) are the memories. Long after the cake and food and people are gone, all you have left are some great memories, if you were able to remember what happened!

The married couple certainly will not remember much of the day. It was such a whirlwind of planning and stress and meeting and greeting. At a large wedding, you will barely remember who was there let alone remember what the heck just happened.

Almost everyone at a wedding brings a camera, and some of the best photos are those captured quickly and candidly. Cell phone shots and selfies are fun memories shared online in one of the many social media type slide shows and on-line albums. These apps can even edit and add fun artistic filters and music for you. Personally, I think those are the best images. But choose your photographer carefully if you want the perfect shots for the wedding album, family keepsakes, and framing.

Go professional

Do not skimp on your precious memories. Friends with cameras who say they would love to shoot your wedding and have an on-line portfolio of their kids and dogs, may not really understand the stress of setting a perfect scene for your framed wall print. Unless they have samples of weddings they have personally photographed, don't go there. To save on the budget, hire the professional for just a few hours of perfect photos then count on guest snapshots to fill in the rest.

If you want more control over guest snaps, disposable cameras that have to come back to you make a great choice. You could also ask your guests not to share wedding photos of you socially until you have posted your own.

Choosing Photographers

Set a reasonable budget for professional photos. You can choose from full service; fully edited, online a print versions, and a beautiful coffee table album. Or, just the photos on a disk without post-production corrections.

Deciding what style of photography speaks to you helps narrow the many choices. If your wedding is a formal affair, in a beautiful church or other grand location, tuxedos, and top hats, the whole nine yards, you might want to consider a classic style, beautifully staged and posed images worthy of a silk-bound album.

If you are running on the beach barefoot without a care in the world, then a candid documentary style might seem the best fit.

Here is a brief description of various styles you might find when researching.

ARTISTIC: This photographer is looking for the light, the composition, and the contrast. They might sit for hours to get the perfect backlight and the perfect pose. They are not so focused on the actual subject as they are in the entire scene. They look at the light, the background, the scenery with you as part of that. You could be a perfect contrast to the backdrop of a tall grove of majestic trees. Poetry!

PHOTOJOURNALIST or LIFESTYLE: They follow the action as it happens and candidly capture many images as they move around, shooting from all angles in all conditions. Some of them staged to look candid, but nonetheless, a relaxed result.

CLASSIC: Formal settings showing an artistic reality in a documentary style that tells a story. Look at your parents or grandparent's photos. Those are classic.

DRAMATIC: These images are straight from the set of Hollywood with dramatic lighting, contrasting colors, or black and white minimalistic scenes. This style takes a special eye, talent, and training.

DOCUMENTARY: Candid and spontaneous events of the day as they happen. Real photos of real life and real people.

Anyone can take great photos, but professionals expect the unexpected. They know how to follow a wedding timeline, make the best of the natural scenery and lighting, and capture every moment and every memory of the day.

Just remember your guests. If you are holding your photo shoot during the cocktail hour, make sure it only takes that one hour to complete.

Kyle and Sara

This lovely 'magazine shoot' looking couple held their wedding in an architecturally historic area of the city. The photographer began with a photo shoot of the groom, posing, and primping and finding the perfect backdrop and lighting. The photographer had two assistants, trying to learn from 'the master'. There were three bags of lenses, lights, batteries, tripods, and other things I did not recognize. Guests with cameras were instructed not to take photos and to move away. One of the assistants was also taking photos from other strange angles. This went on for an hour. Then she started over again with the bride.

After the ceremony, which at this point had already begun late, they went out into the city and did it all again as a couple. That was another two hours at which time the bridal party finally came looking for them. The catering staff was also upset as the food was now ruined, and the guests were starving.

As the videographer, I had already mentioned that photos were taking too long and we should go inside. A sneering look reminded me I was NOT the photographer here and she had a job to do.

This photographer in my opinion, was there for her portfolio. She had the perfect couple in the perfect setting and was not going to waste that. She wanted those perfect shots for herself.

I have experienced many scenarios like this one. The culprits; beautiful looking couples in picturesque scenery who want to feel like models for the day and will just let the photographer dictate the time it takes to do that. There is nothing wrong with that, just remember your guests are waiting for you. Make sure your 'person' keeps the photographers in check and on schedule, so your other vendors and guests are not waiting.

If you want the magazine shoot, plan to do that on another day and dress up again. Who doesn't want to wear that beautiful gown one more time and take to the streets, park, beach, and buildings and spend all day getting the perfect shot? It takes all day to do that. Magazine photographers spend hours and hours setting the perfect scene, and thousands of images later get that one perfectly lit, perfectly smiling, perfectly posed image. Then they Photoshop the life out of it!

Photographers can take up to eight hundred images on one day, thanks to digital, but you might only see about three hundred of the best ones and a couple dozen for the album.

Consider what is important to you and choose your photographer and budget to match. You can spend anywhere from $500 for a disk of about five hundred unedited or semi-edited images, (photographers never want to share their bad photos, and there are always bad ones,) to well over $5000 for the perfect collection in the Italian made coffee table hardcover album.

With photography and videography, it's the editing that takes hours of time. If you want to save money, and have some photo editing experience and time, start with professional photos. You can then edit, crop and get creative and make your album using one of the many online options.

The Cover

The cover photo of this book was a quick thought from the bride as all the girls were getting ready for the day. Hollie suggested the shot and the photographer, Alice, got it in about one take I think. One of those rare moments that just worked so well. It was a fun way to show the essence of the day captured in one scene showing the bride and her entourage's wonderful sense of humor.

Travis and Lindsey

A couple had seen photos of their friend's wedding posted online almost immediately as events were happening, but some of those pictures were not very flattering or in good taste.

For their wedding, just a few weeks later, they asked their guests to refrain from posting photos of the wedding or the couple until they had posted their photos first. The couple released their professional photos one at a time, giving people glimpses of the day. And by the time others could post their own snaps, it had stopped the impulse to upload anything and everything.

Colors

"Even if you don't like colors, you will end up having something red. For everyone who doesn't like color, red is a symbol of a lot of culture. It has a different signification but never a bad one." ~ Christian Louboutin

- ♥ How to NOT have your colors clash with your background
- ♥ How to NOT have your color clash with your attendants
- ♥ How to NOT have online shopping disappointments

With conscious and creative thinking, you can kill the proverbial two birds here. I learned great tips from a very creative and talented photographer, who also was an equally talented florist. She would consult with the couple before their day, encouraging them to choose color wisely with their venue, wedding party, and photos in mind.

If you are going to spend a lot of money on photography, you will want them to be creative and colorful and frame worthy for years to enjoy.

Colors stand out in photos but can equally disappear into the background. The photographer explained that for some reason, white flowers are popular with brides but when you see white flowers against a white dress in a photo, they often disappear, especially at a distance. The florist's bouquet creations were very colorful. Even those who insist on white flowers will have them framed beautifully with colors or beautiful greens and look fabulous against the dress.

Flowers are not the only thing to consider when choosing colors; think of your attendants. It's not often that the girls in a wedding party all look great wearing the same color.

Choosing colors from your computer screen is also a challenge when buying clothes, or anything for that matter, from websites. Make sure you allow plenty of time to order samples. Also, beware the online 'switch.' You might find the perfect designer dress in a magazine or on their website, for more than you want to spend, then after some further research find another company carrying it at a better price. You could be disappointed when it arrives. Off-brand websites will often copy and paste the image of the designer dress for use on their own site. But then send their own unauthorized version. You often do get what you pay for. Use the 'If it's too good to be true...' scenario.

Cori and Brandy

This wedding was in a beautiful old church. The wedding party color theme was red, black, and white. The bridesmaid dresses were red, and the men's black tuxes had red accents to match. The flowers; red for the bride white for the girls. Outside and during a photos session, they all coordinated beautifully, and I could see that the photos would look spectacular. But, as we entered the church, the entire inside was also very red! I mean everything; the carpet, the pews the altar, even the wood trim was reddish, or maybe it was just picking up red from everything else.

The bride stood out against this backdrop well, as you can imagine, but the girls disappeared into the walls and carpet. It was even more evident in the video, which took me some time to color correct in post-production.

Again, picking green for dresses when your wedding is outside on a lawn surrounded by trees will not do much for the photos either. (Unless you choose that green wisely).

I have about five minutes of color film of my parent's wedding from the 1950's and some images my father has since recolored. My mom chose her six bridesmaids and the colors of their dresses to look good in photos. There were two at age five and the same height, two a little older and the same height and the two eldest, the same height so when they all stood together with the bride in the middle the bridesmaids framed her beautifully. No matching groomsmen in those days!

Her colors for that June wedding were lavender, lime, and lemon, and each pair of girls wore one of those colors. If you are into retro weddings, look to the 1950's for some beautiful ideas.

Jess and Aimee

I recently attended a wedding where the bridesmaids all wore colors that each matched a different flower in the bride's bouquet. The groomsmen also had the same mixed and matching ties and pocket squares. As the wedding party gathered together, posed for photos, or just casually chatting, the creative mix of these vibrant colors was even more stunning.

To Video or Not to Video

A recent survey from the Videographers Association said that of all the couples that did not have a video of their wedding, 60% wished they had.

When I consult with couples about capturing their day, they often explain, they don't like seeing themselves in a video, and don't want the intrusion of a camera in their face all day. It could be that your only experience with wedding video is what gets passed around the internet; the bloopers, the blunders, and fainting best man! I have been to weddings when the cameras are in your face, and they are big and intrusive and too close for comfort. But like photography, you choose what you want in a videographer. If you want the Hollywood movie, they will get up close and personal. But, if you just want to capture a few moments, relive the vows you will not remember saying, or catch a few guests wishing you well, look for the 'fly on the wall' camera team. Unless you want to play to the lens and have fun with it, you will not even know they are there.

Many people share the fact that they have a video of their wedding and have never watched it. It sits on a VHS or DVD in the closet. I like to explain that it's not for you to watch in one year or five years, it's the history that you can share fifty years from now if you store and preserve that video well. You must have experienced the joy of looking at old photos from your grandparent's day. It will be the same for your grandchildren many years from now.

For my parents 60th anniversary, I took the fifteen minutes of 35 mm film, converted it to digital, added some special effects and filters and cleaned it up. I can't tell you how many times we have enjoyed watching those few minutes of long gone relatives.

Today, of course, there is the 'cell phone' video coverage. You can't seem to go anywhere or do anything without ending up on YouTube.

You can make some great video from cell phone footage if the person shooting knows a little of what they are doing. Phones are perfect for short clips and an occasional funny or poignant moment, but for full-length coverage of your day, and all those special moments, you need a professional videographer. Cameras that shoot in low light and have excellent sound recording capabilities. New technology makes it easy to create a finished piece, but you also need the time and patience to edit all that footage.

I think the main reason a lot of people do not like to have video footage of themselves is a little like why they don't like to see themselves in photos.

For video, it's a bit different. You don't just pose and smile you are captured in your full glory, warts and all! Professional editing can remove the not so flattering scenes, just as the photographer can edit the blemishes from your face. But if you want a full-length documentary of your entire wedding, and you want it to be entertaining, remember a few tricks before the camera is rolling.

- ♥ Don't pose. Don't pull the 'selfie face' or be 'on' all day because you know the camera is watching.
- ♥ Relax, just be yourself and ignore the cameras.
- ♥ Talk into the camera to whoever you think is watching; your betrothed, your family, yourself twenty years from now. Your future children. Have fun.
- ♥ Don't chew gum or anything for that matter. There is nothing worse than seeing people chewing during a lovely romantic moment. For breath freshness, pop a mint.

Video Friends

We were asked to edit some video footage that a friend had taken as a favor for the couple. He was not a professional but had, what they thought was a decent enough camera. When we received the footage, the quality was very grainy because the camera was not capable of compensating for low light areas. The scenes were shaky and the voices were unrecognizable. We did manage to get creative with some of the footage and lay a music track over the bad audio, but none of the vows could be heard and many of the toasts and well-wishes were lost.

Timing

"The key is not to prioritize what's on your schedule, but to schedule your priorities."

~Stephen Covey

- ♥ How to NOT become overwhelmed
- ♥ How to NOT underestimate a detailed timeline
- ♥ How to NOT lose your guests

All projects need a schedule. Wedding planning books all have the obligatory checklists of when things should be done; venue; a year, wedding dress; six months, save the dates and invitations, etc. Then there is the timeline for the day-of.

If you have done your homework and studied the wedding planning bibles, you will at least have a calendar of some sort to start with. Type A's will have every movement from waking to sleep in fifteen-minute intervals listing all vendors and who oversees what, plus has ten copies for everyone. Perfect. Then there are the 'not so specific' types who will state the show-up time, the ceremony times and reception. Then hope everyone just gets there on time!

Wherever you are in the timing world, do not underestimate how long it takes to get things done, or how other people's time clocks work.

The more people you are planning and working with, the more you need to add a margin of time to accommodate them.

Alejandro and Kara

I was hired to video an entire day, everything from the getting ready to the leaving. A good 10 hours. We had a ceremony start time of 5:00 PM. The bride wanted us to capture the families getting ready, some pre-ceremony photos, of the bridal party 'hanging out,' and the 'first look.' We suggested our arrival be about three hours before the ceremony to allow for set up. The goal was to get just enough of the getting ready before the dress went on and the groom saw the bride for the first time.

The venue was a large single story home with beautiful gardens often used for weddings. The bride was handling all the planning herself, and both families were helping. We were given a verbal timeline for the day. She informed everyone to arrive by 2:00 PM to help get everything ready. The 'girls' would come with hair and makeup done, so they could just get dressed and assist the bride and be ready for photos by 3:00 PM.

Alejandro and his party were told to arrive by 3:00 PM also dressed and ready for pictures, then greet guests. Someone was picking up the keg and ice along the way and other family members were coming with food and decorations.

We arrived a little earlier than 2:00 PM as the location was quite remote and we did not want to be late. Kara and a couple of her 'girls' had also arrived a little early and were already stressed because the venue did not have anything set up. She assumed that she would walk in and the place would be beautiful and decorated. Just as the photos showed in the marketing materials. She was already in tears when I arrived.

What to NOT do #1. Do not arrive earlier than your assigned time because you just get in the way of the set-up team.

The staff had also just arrived and was already getting to work, doing what they needed to do, and were not at all worried about the time.

I reassured the Kara and sent her to start getting ready. By 3:00 PM, the rest of the wedding party, had still not arrived. More tears. Most of the wedding party, I found out, were on the groom's side. So were most of the family who was helping with the decorating and food. Kara was assured that they were on their way, but she underestimated how his family worked together.

Meanwhile, the photographer had also arrived expecting to start his photography session.

What to NOT do #2. Do not assume that others work in the same time zone as you.

We all know the friends and family members who are consistently late to everything and have no concept of time. Make sure you have a detailed timeline, and everyone has a copy. Then make sure that someone is holding someone else accountable for being where they are supposed to be, on time. That should NOT be the Bride!

The girls finally arrived ninety minutes late, followed by those with all the food and decorations. No one had any hair or makeup done and did not seem at all concerned that they were late. Amidst a lot of family conversation, laughter and fun, things started getting done. It was clearly obvious that this family worked at their own pace, without regard for the clock.

By 4:00 PM, the girls were still no closer to being ready. The photographer, my second camera operator, and I had been sitting and waiting for over four hours and still had not captured anything. The officiant was due to arrive any minute. Hopefully, he did not have a later appointment!

Kara again was in tears as nothing at this point was going as she planned. The family, with all the food and decorations, were no closer to being ready for the ceremony. They were too busy in the kitchen, and the girls were still playing with hair and makeup. The trouble was, no one else really knew what the plans were, and no one was keeping track of the time, except the Bride.

Feeling sorry for her and wanting to get this wedding started, I stepped in. I spoke with the distraught bride and asked if I could help, and with a sigh of relief she gave up the day to me. My planner hat went on, and with some quick delegations most everyone just followed my directions and things got underway. The ceremony was an hour late but still an hour earlier than if we just let things happen without a plan.

Get your checklist and make your timeline and make sure EVERYONE has a copy. But my advice on what to NOT do would be to not stick to it so religiously that you go crazy trying to keep to it. You must, at least, have a margin of error in there for those moments you don't anticipate. I always start from the end of the day and work backward, adding the non-movable times, like the ceremony, first.

Let's do an example for the ground zero part of your one or two-year timeline.

You want your ceremony to begin at 4:00 PM and your venue requires an 11:00 PM end. Several factors will determine what time you should arrive, such as where you are getting ready and what time you have access to the venue, but make sure you plan to get there on time to get married, and that everything you have planned in between will happen by 11:00 PM.

There are dozens of different combinations of what a typical day might look like, but we will use my timeline estimates in the table following.

Plug in your important events, then work back from there, estimating how long each section or task will take. Within your estimation remember to add the margin of error.

Typical Wedding Day Timeline	Estimate Time
DRESSING & PREPARATIONS	**2 - 3 Hours**
Getting Ready and Other Preparations	60 min
First Look / Bride & Groom Photos	30 min
Wedding Party Photos	30 min
CEREMONY	**1 hour**
Processional	15 min
Ceremony	20 min
Recessional and Certificate Signing	15 min
POST CEREMONY	**1 hour**
Family Photography Session	30 min
Cocktail Reception	1 hr
RECEPTION (3 - 5 hrs)	**3 - 5 hours**
Dinner Service	60 min
Toasts and Speeches	20 min
Cake Cutting and Service	10 min
First & Family Dances	10 min
Bouquet & Garter Toss	15 min
Dancing & Celebrating	whatever time is left

I use these margins for:

- ♥ People moving; are they all able to walk at a normal pace or do you have elderly or physically challenged guests? Do your friends and family like to chat? It's very hard to break up a good conversation!
- ♥ Number of guests; It's easier to get fifty people to arrive, find a seat and actually sit, than one hundred and fifty. The larger the crowd, the more time needed.
- ♥ Traffic moving; including parking and having to walk or hike somewhere. Is there parking nearby? Will guests

need to find a parking lot or street parking? Are you arranging a shuttle?
- ♥ Weather; people walk faster to get out of the cold and rain but love to stroll slower on a beautiful, warm, sunny day.

It's amazing how some of these little things can add ten or fifteen minutes to your schedule.

If you add the margin, you will either be early and have time to relax. Or, not have so much time to sit around, but not worry about getting off schedule.

Plug in the non-movable times, list your events around that. Create a spreadsheet, (use mine as a guide) so you can easily add and move events and times as you need to. Then estimate how long you think each element of your day will take, do some math, add a margin and voila! Timeline.

So now you have a little idea of how a day might go. Of course, you can add new events and remove elements of the day you do not need, but from the guest and vendor perspective, keeping things tight and on a schedule helps them plan and saves you money.

The Waiting Game

I cannot tell you how many weddings I have been to where the guests are sitting around waiting. Waiting for the ceremony, waiting for the couple to show up, (from a photo session mostly, remember Kyle and Sara's story?) so they can eat dinner, (the caterers are also often waiting). Waiting makes for a very boring wedding. When you are not paying attention, you will lose your guests, just like a boring movie or play will lose its audience.

You also need to make sure your guests know where to go next. Having a program or order of service helps them anticipate the next part of your day. Or just a few announcements from the DJ helps. Always have refreshments when they get from the ceremony to reception, even if it's just water and soft drinks, it makes waiting just a little more tolerable.

If you keep things to a schedule, or add some fun activities to your day, like a photo booth, guests will not feel like they are being kept waiting, if you really need to take more photos.

I have seen some pretty creative entertainment while guests are enjoying the cocktail hour. They range from magicians to Polynesian fire dancers and belly dancing. Have some fun and entertain your guests. They will remember all the extra attention over waiting for you.

During the reception as dinner is wrapping up and you have a captive audience, go right into the speeches and toasts. I also like to see the cake cutting and first dance here. It is another time during the day where you should be thinking of your guests and vendors, not you.

While you are enjoying your first dance, the caterers are cutting the rest of the cake and serving it. If you are not having the traditional cake and opting for a dessert table, have the DJ announce that it is now open for their enjoyment. People will also feel like this is the appropriate time to leave if they need to.

The Food

"I don't like food that's too carefully arranged; it makes me think that the chef is spending too much time arranging and not enough time cooking. If I wanted a picture I'd buy a painting".
~Andy Rooney

- ♥ How to NOT assume all vendors are overcharging just because it's a wedding
- ♥ How to NOT end up with wasted food
- ♥ How to NOT presume you are the only event on the vendor's calendar for that day (especially food)

I hear this comment all the time, "We are being overcharged just because it's a wedding." Truthfully, having dealt with couples who obsess over details and are constantly changing things, I think there should be 'battle pay' involved! However, what you will find are vendors who reduce rates for mid-week, and off-season events, or trimming the menu.

Supply and demand have always dictated costs of goods and services. Weddings are not usually scheduled mid-week, but it's the best time if you want a good deal.

Wasted Food

I cannot count how much food I see wasted at weddings. People just do not seem to eat that much. Now, if the wedding party includes six guys from the football team and several of their friends are invited, then yes, they will go through about three servings each. But, for the most part, there is a lot of waste.

Buffets are the culprit. The menu includes your proteins, a pasta dish, some sides, bread, salad, and a fruit plate for your 150 guests, but not everyone eats everything, so you have lots of waste. Then, because you saw it at a friend's wedding or on Pinterest, you want to have a fancy dessert/candy table, chocolate fountain and/or coffee cart.

The Wedding Cake

Another extra expense to all those food choices that is often leftover is the cake. Probably by about 50% I would guess from all the cake I have seen thrown away. You must have the cake, right? It's tradition, right? Plus, they look pretty on display. You need the photo of the cake-in-the-face. It's all part of the fun and expected by the photographer and after the family toasts. It's what sends you on your merry way. But, do you need to throw away about $200 of sugary flowers? If not, choose wisely and consider your venue.

Will you be inside, protected from the elements or outside where it's susceptible to the wind, the sun, bugs, or curious little fingers? Make sure you tell your bakery where the cake will be sitting for those few hours so they can plan the icing accordingly. You also need to plan accordingly. Once the cake arrives and has been set up, you cannot easily move it, nor would you want to.

Trending now is trays of fancy cupcakes and specialty drinks. I was recently at a wedding where the dessert table looked lovely. It was themed and decorated beautifully, but was untouched by the end of the evening. The hosts were trying to get guests to take it home. Your body can only handle so much sugar in one night, and most of that will come from the alcohol. So, cut back on the desserts if anything. After a night of drinking, a giant popcorn machine or onsite gourmet popcorn vendor will be your best friend. It's also an excellent way to soak up all that alcohol before your guests all hit the road!

Rob and Janey

> I was waiting for the wedding party to return from the ceremony and start the party at an outside venue on a warm summer day. The baker had arrived and was setting up the cake in its designated location. It was the most beautiful cake I had ever seen. Three tiers supported by champagne glasses and covered in flowers. He spent a long time setting up the table stacking the layers and decorating the cake. It looked perfect. He then went off to prepare whatever else he was preparing.

> I was standing many feet away, and as I admired the masterpiece in icing, it started to slowly slide sideways. I could not get to the cake or the baker in time to save it, and no one else ever saw it in one piece. Not even a photo!!

At about $1.50 to $12.00 per slice, order your cake to feed just fifty to seventy-five percent of your guests. It can be cut into smaller sizes since most people don't eat it all anyway. Of all the cake, I have tasted over the years, only a few of them would I choose to eat again.

If you want to show off an artfully designed six-tiered cake, make just the bottom layer real and the rest prop. You might still be paying for all the decorating but can save on the cake itself. Many large cakes are like that in case you didn't know! No one will know once it's all cut up.

Alternatives to the traditional cake (and some have been done to death already) are:

- ♥ Cupcakes
- ♥ Pies (great for the garden, farm or picnic type weddings)

- ♥ Cookie table
- ♥ Mixed dessert table
- ♥ Ice cream bar (especially in the summer and outdoors)
- ♥ And a plethora of ideas on Pinterest!

If you do opt for a dessert table, keep it simple. Rather than have waste, put some to-go boxes on the table and have your guests grab some goodies for the trip home. Checkout your local supply store or my favorite place for anything; Amazon! Print some 'Thank You for Coming' stickers, and your guests will love it.

Food Tasting

Many couples go food tasting and choose their menu based on what they like. The trouble is, you have about 150 different tastes on the guest list. Also, you are sampling food prepared for you in a small batch by appointment, not made for a hundred guests, sometimes in a tent. Also, it might be late being served because you are off having photos taken.

Choose a caterer based on reviews, personal experience, and by the type of food you would like to serve your guests.

Don't think you have to choose what is on their traditional menu. Chefs like a challenge and maybe they would like to create a menu based on your culinary heritage. You could share some family traditions and dishes with your guests. Personally, I love a good old English roast dinner. But I am also a lover of Indian food. Delicacies from an exotic country where you vacation, or a selection of international hors d'oeuvres that fit everyone's tastes, will mix up the traditional buffet.

Venues that do not have onsite catering often have a list of 'preferred' vendors they insist you choose from, limiting your options. If there is a venue you would like to use, you might want to check out their catering options first. All preferred or favorite commercial catering companies are comparable in quality and food. It will be your menu choices, salmon over chicken for example or appetizer selections with fancy names, that change the costs, and you often do get what you pay for. What would your guests enjoy the most?

Ingenious Alternatives

Food carts are all very popular today and not exclusive to festivals, fairs and Cartlandia's! It's an excellent choice for the casual outside wedding where the venue may not have a kitchen or catering options. The food can be cooked to order and prepared fresh on site. If you want to bring in more than one choice of food, you can.

Search the Internet for hundreds of ideas, but consider adding 'sides' to a main course cart service. Think hotdogs, pretzels, ice cream, coffee carts, and popcorn machines.

Remember, though, food carts do not come with servers and clean up staff unless they also offer full catering. Make sure you include some hired catering staff to help with table setup and tear down and the cleanup of all the mess.

To Drink or Not to Drink

- ♥ How to NOT feel like you have to pay for alcohol
- ♥ How to NOT have your wedding party over imbibe
- ♥ How to NOT let you guests down during 'cocktail hour'

Guests do like to drink and have an excellent time, especially if it's free and there is no reason to foot the cost of free drinks for everyone. I have been to many 'dry' weddings, and there is much discussion on wedding boards about it. Sometimes the decision is for the budget, some for religious reasons. For the majority, it seems, they want to at least toast the happy couple with a good wine or champagne.

I also find that today, guests are drinking less for lots of reasons and the parents are the ones who want to host the bar. Dad won't be happy without his Old Fashion, or mom likes her Martini, but there is nothing wrong with limiting your bar to beer and wine only or cutting the drinks off early. Try offering non-alcoholic and wine cocktails, there are many ideas online for those. It also cuts down on the 'over drinkers' who tend to get a little too rowdy at the end of the night.

If you want to offer drink options, have a no-host bar. If guests have to pay for alcohol, they will drink less.

And don't get me started on the pre-celebration drinks! I have escorted many a best man or bridesmaid from the wedding because of too much pre-partying!

The Bar Tab

While bartending for a huge wedding at a five-star resort one weekend, the father of the bride hosted the bar for the night, but he failed to set a limit on the tab, or maybe he was not that bothered about the costs, and the guests took advantage. It took just four hours to reach a bar tab of $25,000!

The Music

"If music be the food of love, play on".

~William Shakespeare

- ♥ How to NOT deafen your guests
- ♥ How to NOT miss a beat
- ♥ How to NOT think your phone is a DJ

A couple recently asked me; "DJ or live band?" I had to think about that because there are pros and cons to both. For most events, I book the type of entertainment based on the event and audience I am trying to please. It is important to remember that criteria and not on what I personally enjoy. For your wedding, you are choosing for you, but please keep your guests in mind too. They might not appreciate three hours of heavy metal or rap! A good dance cover band is generally the best choice. You can always load up your phone with some rap or heavy metal to play during their break.

I also love a great DJ. You get to choose the song you want to hear, for the most part, and they have just about any genre you can ask for. Like bands, there are great and not so great DJ's. I have worked with some very boring DJ's and some over the top energetic and love to hear their own voice, types.

What I don't like to see and do not advocate for is the do-it-yourself phone or music player hooked to a bluetooth speaker!

Dominic and Ana

This couple decided that an iPod would be the music of choice at their reception, to save the cost of a DJ. They had planned for Dominic's best friend to manage the music and loaded the device with all their favorite tunes. They hooked it up to a set of large home speakers and tested it before all the guests arrived. It played happily during the cocktail hour and dinner. It was good background music.

But when time came for the toasts and first dance, poor planning was becoming apparent. Without a real DJ and a professional DJ set up, they now did not have a microphone for the toasts or to announce the first dance. Luckily, those giving toasts had loud voices, but they did have to shout just a little too much.

For the first dance, the friend with the music could not be found, and when he did appear, he took a little too much time scrolling the small screen for the correct song.

As the guests started filling the dance floor, it was clear that the home speakers were just not powerful enough to blast a good dance sound through the crowd and into the large room.

Nick and Mandy

When a live band does work.

Nick and Mandy were dance instructors and had a huge dance following. They hired one of our most popular, nationally acclaimed, and famous swing dance bands. The reception was in a huge dance hall with a full professional dance floor and the wedding party performed an amazingly choreographed dance routine for their guests. The band was loud, to say the least, but because they were in such a large venue there were plenty of places for guests to go to protect their hearing. (If I have to stand near a loud band for a few hours, I always wear ear plugs or sound restricting headphones, your guests might not think about that.)

Bailey and Kelly

When a live band does NOT work.

This reception was in a small venue and the band, friends of the couple, offered to play for free. The room had terrible acoustics, and the sound system was awful. I am not sure if it was the band's equipment or came with the facility, but rather than lower the levels to accommodate the weak speakers and the small room, they cranked them up and distorted. Guests left early or were mostly outside, and Bailey was disappointed that no one was dancing.

From experience, I recommend a DJ at least during the early part of your day. They will set up your sound for the ceremony so your guests can hear what is being said. They can also play softer background music for your guest arrivals, cocktails, and dinner. They will also cue the correct songs at the exact time, and keep your day on time. I work with the DJ to make sure the timeline stays on time.

If you want a live band, start with the DJ from ceremony through dinner, then schedule for the band to start their first set after the toasts, with the first dance.

Other Music

Many couples love a string quartet, soloist, harpist, or other gentler performance for guest arrivals and ceremony music. Again, consider the venue. If you are outside, strings are very hard to hear if there is no amplification. Most of these musicians do not come with speaker systems. Check with them when booking. A solo acoustic guitar is impossible to hear on a beach, for example. Those closest and maybe the officiant will hear the music, but that is about all. I have been on beaches where the musician will bring a small portable speaker just enough to hear from the back row.

Do consider your venue when choosing your music. And do find a professional. A good DJ, with pre-planning, can accommodate for these conditions and your guests will appreciate it.

Relationships

"I have great hopes that we shall love each other all our lives as
much as if we had never married at all."

— Lord Byron

I love weddings where all the family members get involved. A wedding should be a family event, not the overdone commercial money driven production it has become.

But, you also have those family dynamics!

Great big (especially European) families all love to cook their traditional dishes, will offer to do all the food and probably make way too much! It's an excellent idea because you're all chipping in. If your family loves to cook, and offers to cook, let them cook. Let them bring on their magic. Then, hire somebody to serve, to clean up, and put it all away. The truth is, if left to the family, that won't get done, or will begrudgingly.

Your guests, even the family, should not be expected to do all the cleaning. I've been there, done that, cleaned up an entire wedding because the family thought they were helping by 'catering' all the food.

Greg and Shannon

Greg's dear friends were restaurant owners (very different from event catering by the way) and offered, as their gift, to provide all the food for the reception. Their offer was to cook, deliver, set up and serve the guests. Wonderful. Saves a ton of money, right?

However, the wedding venue had very strict vendor policies in place, for very good reason; you use their preferred and trusted vendors, or you do not rent the facility. The couple pleaded with the sales team to be able to use someone outside of their 'approved vendors', with promises of professional services and clean up. To the facilities' chagrin, they allowed it.

Because they had to keep their business open, the chef hired extra serving staff, so they were not pulling from the restaurant.

Problem #1; some of the temporarily hired staff didn't show up.

Problem #2; as soon as everyone was eating, the temporary staff left. I think even the restaurant owner left early to get back to the restaurant for the dinner shift.

Problem #3; no one was left to clean up. That was not part of the 'gift deal'. The gift was the food and the service, not the cleanup and the bride and groom obviously didn't think to consider that part.

Shannon hired me just the day before the wedding, after realizing she needed help to manage some of the day-of planning. When I asked about the catering service she hired, I assumed everything was included, from delivery to clean up. My lesson; don't assume!

Problem #4, when you have catering staff you also have someone experienced in cutting a wedding cake! As the catering staff for this event all left during dinner, there was no one left to cut the cake. After some great toasts and posed photos of cake cutting, everyone looked to everyone else to cut and serve! There was not even a knife left!

Luckily, I have cut many cakes, but that was not my job. Neither was the cleanup and taking out the garbage. Plan ahead and hire professionals if you don't want your guests doing the dishes.

The bride and groom had left before the rest of the guests, and to this day I am sure they have no idea that just two of their guests had to clean up their mess.

Dave and Jenny

"My Big Fat Greek Wedding" was one way to describe this blending of two very different cultures. Dave's smaller gathering of estranged parents and college friends vs. Jenny's large, noisy, multigenerational, and overly helpful family. They have done this before; large family gatherings, food, visiting, laughing, chatting, having a grand old time in a large kitchen with free-flowing tequila! It's not planned; it's just what they do. 'Yaya' directs the women down to the smallest girl to shop, cook, bake, prepare, deliver, unwrap and serve. The men are banned from the kitchen to get the beer, soda, ice, BBQ and whatever else. Everyone has their job, and they all know what to do. It's just magical. As long as you are not worried about the time it takes them to get all that done! And yes, they all cleaned up too.

These weddings do not run on a timetable! Things happen when they happen, and you have to go with the flow.

Unless you have a big fat anything family, you don't plan a family 'potluck' wedding, unless you plan it well.

If you want the casual outdoor wedding where the family brings the food potluck style, great. I love that. My wedding was like that. But hire a cleanup crew. Or at the least, hire temporary catering staff to help with the 'dirty work.' Let your family enjoy the day. Even if they insist they 'have got this,' don't let them. No one wants to stay late after a fun day of partying to clean the up. Let them go away remember the great day they had celebrating with you.

The Preparations

"It's important to still look like yourself on your wedding day, so I didn't do anything drastic: —Lily Aldridge

Here is where I think it's all about the bride for a change! Get your girls and celebrate. In many cultures, preparing the bride for her matrimony and new life is a fun and exciting part of the day, or week in some cultures!

Whatever type of wedding you are planning, carve out some special time for your friends, your mother, grandmother, and whoever those special ladies in your life are. Plan a spa day, hair and makeup just before getting dressed. Having a cocktail or a light lunch and a good laugh together lightens the planning. It is a time for you to give up on the details and relax so you can enjoy your day.

And the men too!

The men too can have this prep day. Nothing wrong with a spa treatment, hanging at the sports bar, or even a day of surfing the waves.

While the ladies are sipping tea and the guys are playing their games, just remember to have someone watch the clock. Everyone tends to be enjoying the time a little too much and forgets when to be ready for photos or even the ceremony!

The Dress

"When I decided to get married at 40, I couldn't find a dress with the modernity or sophistication I wanted. That's when I saw the opportunity for a wedding gown business."

—Vera Wang

- ♥ How to NOT say 'Yes to the Dress' too soon
- ♥ How to NOT assume you will fit in the dress
- ♥ How to NOT disappear in photos

The dress is all about the bride.

Whether the bride wears the traditional wedding gown, or a simple summer dress or even a good pair of jeans, she wants to be the focal point of the event, the prettiest person in the room.

You don't have to get sucked into the expense of the big fluffy white dress. I was never one to want 'the dress,' and you are not required to go all out and wear something you don't want to.

The tradition of the white gown for a wedding goes back hundreds of years, and Queen Victoria made it fashionable, so all the girls of that era had to copy her. Just like today, whatever the latest fashion mags, celebrity or princess choose to wear, that is what you will see in all the bridal marketing.

Don't say 'Yes to the Dress' until you sleep on it. You will wear this only one day. Okay, so it will live on in infamy in photos and video, hopefully. But, do we need to spend more than $1000 on a dress you will wear once? You can find some great deals in the wedding dress industry with a little research, not to mention in the rental and used departments.

Look for evening wear too. There are some lovely gowns that are not considered wedding dresses, therefore, keeping the costs down. And, who said you have to wear white?

My wedding dress was a prom dress and on the sale rack for $30! Looked like a wedding dress to me, but labeled and priced as a prom dress. If you are crafty or can sew, you can personalize it with custom details. If it needs professional altering to fit better, it will still be a bargain.

Bridal shops have sales all the time, but don't be dissuaded if they don't look perfect. By the end of the wedding day, most dresses don't look perfect anyway. Shop with an open mind.

Many of the dresses on sale are the samples from the store. They will probably need a good cleaning and alternations. You can pick up an expensive designer dress for less than $100 if you are a savvy shopper.

Borrowing a friend's dress or finding one in a consignment shop needs the same consideration. Understand what can be done to the dress to make it work for you. Most wedding dresses are made to alter relatively easy. Some can be adjusted to fit, some not so much. Have someone with dress making or alteration experience look at it on you before you decide to borrow or buy it, to avoid a day of disaster.

Brandy

Another day of shooting video at a wedding while the bride was getting ready. The dress was hanging up in the dressing room, so I adjusted it for a better angle. I noticed that the size label showed size ten which worried me a little, as the bride was clearly somewhere between an eighteen and twenty-two!

I have altered and fit and made from scratch, dozens of wedding dresses. I knew this dress should never have been considered by the bride, or by whoever sold it to her. She went on to explain how she came to get the dress, 'at a low price,' and argued that because it laced up at the back and was sleeveless, there was room to 'let it out.' This is so not true! Yes, we did get most of her into the dress, but I am not sure how she could breathe. There was a lot of her, in a little of it.

Just because a dress laces at the back, does not mean you can adjust it four sizes.

The bride always wants to look her best for her groom, (but mostly to show off to her friends and look good in photos). Dress up and look beautiful, but be comfortable and realistic.

We have all seen too many brides pass out in 'funny home movies' because they wanted to cinch that waist in one more inch! No one will notice that one inch, but they will certainly pay attention when you turn blue or your boobs pop out during a great dance routine! (Yes, I have seen that too).

If you obtain a dress that you don't have to return or pay for, then you can spend a little more on alterations.

Catherine

Catherine was girl getting married on a very slim budget. She was offered an exquisite designer dress if she could make it work and brought it to me for advice. I managed to recut it from a size twelve to a six. It turned out so lovely and one of my best remakes. But you cannot always go the other way.

Don't try and get into a dress that is smaller than one size down, no matter what the price. And don't think that you will lose enough weight before the wedding. We all dream that one! Larger sizes are easier to take down, but you can't always add what is not there. Well, you can sometimes. I have made dresses work for girls who have suddenly found themselves several months pregnant after the purchase of the dress, but it is a lot of work.

The bridesmaid dresses are another nightmare for some. Often the bride knows how she would like to see her attendants look, or has drooled over another perfect magazine spread. In marketing photos, all the girls are the same height, weight, and all look magazine perfect. In real life, your ladies are all shapes and sizes and do not all look their best in strapless fitted satin fuchsia!

Some options are to find a style of dress that looks good on all shapes, and let them pick one shade from your color theme. If this is a casual garden wedding, for instance, and your theme is spring with light pastels, have one girl in each spring color. Match your flowers for example. (read Jess and Aimee's story.)

To complement each attendant's figure, pick a color and have the girls find the dress that works for them.

Don't underestimate the classic black dress. These look good on everyone. With the right flowers to pop some color and a bright, colorful pair of shoes with a matching wrap, the girls will look great and have a dress they can wear again.

Beware of online ordering. It is hard to see colors and determine if their listed sizes match your measurements.

Hollie

Hollie found a lovely dress for her girls online at a reasonable price and ordered a sample. The dress arrived and seemed perfect so she ordered the rest. When they arrived, maybe a couple of weeks before the wedding, she found that they had switched the original sample for cheaper fabrics and shoddy work, or just sent the wrong ones. Hollie was devastated, and with just two weeks before the wedding was scrambling to get her money back and find new dresses.

By all means, shop around, but know where you are getting your dresses from. Know the return policy and leave plenty of time for corrections.

Alternatives

"It's not the number of people who attend, the location of the ceremony, or the words that are spoken, but the love that is shared".

~ Lesley Wise

I can see why couples feel the need to host a wedding in the fanciest (and expensive) places. They make you feel special for a day. You can pretend for that one moment nothing else matters, that you are the queen of the castle, the icing on the cake. Then, you come back down to earth, and the rest of life is just plain boring, even to the point that you might regret your marriage. It happens!

But if you are the average person, (one that must watch every penny, and does not have a trust fund to tap) and average people would be reading this book, why spend a few thousand on a historic ballroom or fancy winery. A place you might never have been before and will never go to again, (unless for another wedding).

If the venue has no real meaning other than you saw it in a bridal magazine photo shoot, or that you want the perfect photos, rethink what is meaningful to you and what your budget can handle.

If you are royalty, I can understand that a 600-year-old cathedral would be fitting. If you go to church regularly, then, of course, you will use your church. If you work or own a historic building, you might like to take advantage of that option. But, if your life together is spent hiking wooded trails, get married on a wooded trail, or at least in a park. Find a place where you and your family and friends would enjoy being with you the most.

Beyond the Church

The need for a religious ceremony doesn't have to mean Church! Many religious people are spiritually inspired out in nature, or in their home. You can bring your preacher, minister, Father, or pastor with you to your place of wedding worship.

I once attended the most fun and enlightened Catholic wedding at a mountaintop winery. It was lively and fun, and very funny. This thoroughly modern Catholic priest had a great sense of humor, quite a contrast to the traditional priests I have encountered in the past.

Beyond the 'Wedding Venue'

If it's difficult to find your dream venue, consider asking a friend who has a large piece of property. Just because it's not on any of the wedding venue lists doesn't mean it's not out there. Places you least expect can become beautiful wedding sites.

If you are looking at public places, parks, gardens, bridges, you will have to do some research. Many public places do not let you hold an 'organized gathering' of more than six or so people without a permit. Of course, you can always take your chances at a quiet spot, and hold a quick ceremony before anyone notices. But, check around first before you get excited. Go to the local Visitor Centers and Chamber of Commerce.

Many people are not aware of all the beautiful and inexpensive places to hold a memorable wedding.

Elopements

Elopements are the most romantic of weddings I think. Back in the day, couples who wanted to wed quickly and in secret would run away together, most often against the wishes of thier parents. They found a small church and the local preacher who would do the honors for a few coins.

Today, elopements are more planned. They are smaller ceremonies with just a few guests held just about anywhere you can gather an officiant and a couple of witnesses; City Hall, small gardens, local parks, beaches, and boats. Elopements are perfect for the destination wedding when there is just the couple taking a romantic vacation.

Still, there is a certain amount of planning that needs to happen. Even if it's to just jump in the car and drive, you still need gas, food, and money, and to get a license. Unless you are lucky enough to know a friend, who can legally sign your documents, you also often need to pay the person performing the ceremony.

When there is drama with family and friends, and you can't decide on your guest list, then elopement might be your best friend. There is nothing wrong with taking off for a secret rendezvous, then arranging for a party sometime later. But don't think that you have actually to throw an expensive party. Sometimes a potluck BBQ or just dinner with your closest friends is all you need to share your moment.

Beyond the Normal

Well, nothing and nowhere is normal anymore. My normal may not be your normal. We see weddings in all shapes and sizes and places. There are no rules. There are no expectations, for the most part. There doesn't even need to be a ceremony or party. The necessities are the couple, the officiant, witnesses, and signatures.

But we love lavish affairs anyway. We love tradition. We love to be the same and to be different. We love to dress up, or down, and prepare for our new life, our next chapter, our new family.

However you chose to celebrate this wonderful tradition, do it with love and understanding and compassion.

If you would like to download either of the worksheets, or have other questions during your planning journey, please visit my website www.itsnotaboutthebride.com

Thank you for reading along. I hope you learned at least one thing to NOT do!

Happy Planning!

48133276R00068

Made in the USA
San Bernardino, CA
17 April 2017